Teacher's Survival Guide

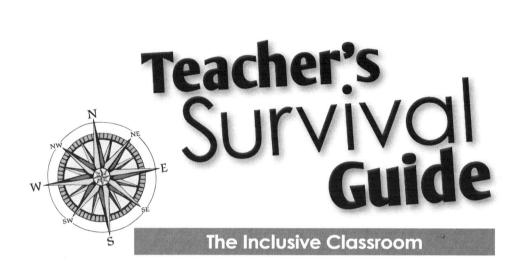

The Inclusive Classroom

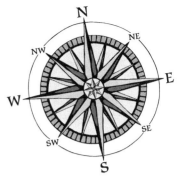

Teacher's Survival Guide

The Inclusive Classroom

Cynthia G. Simpson, Ph.D., Vicky G. Spencer, Ph.D., and Jeffrey P. Bakken, Ph.D.

PRUFROCK PRESS INC.
WACO, TEXAS

Dedications

To our families and colleagues who support and motivate us to meet the individual needs of all students with disabilities.

To all preservice teachers and teachers already in the field who strive to meet the educational, social, and emotional needs of all students with disabilities in inclusive classrooms and all other educational environments.

Library of Congress Cataloging-in-Publication Data

Simpson, Cynthia G.
Teacher's survival guide : the inclusive classroom / Cynthia G. Simpson, Vicky G. Spencer, Jeffrey P. Bakken.
    p. cm.
Includes bibliographical references.
ISBN 978-1-59363-541-1 (pbk.)
1. Inclusive education. 2. Special education. 3. Active learning. 4. Activity programs in education. I. Spencer, Vicky G. II. Bakken, Jeffrey P. III. Title.

LB1027.23.S57 2011
371.9'046--dc22

2011009005

Edited by Lacy Compton

Layout Design by Raquel Trevino

ISBN-13: 978-1-59363-541-1

Printed in the United States of America.

At the time of this book's publication, all facts and figures cited are the most current available. All telephone numbers, addresses, and website URLs are accurate and active. All publications, organizations, websites, and other resources exist as described in the book, and all have been verified. The authors and Prufrock Press Inc. make no warranty or guarantee concerning the information and materials given out by organizations or content found at websites, and we are not responsible for any changes that occur after this book's publication. If you find an error, please contact Prufrock Press Inc.

Prufrock Press Inc.
P.O. Box 8813
Waco, TX 76714-8813
Phone: (800) 998-2208
Fax: (800) 240-0333
http://www.prufrock.com

Table of Contents

Acknowledgements

A special thanks to all of the teachers who contributed to the survival secrets of teachers by sharing their own experiences as they began their teaching careers. Also, thank you to Laura Harris, doctoral student at George Mason University, for assisting in the editing process of this manuscript.

Introduction

Special education is a dynamic and growing field of study and requires teachers to have expertise in a wide variety of areas. It also requires teachers to be flexible, creative, and collaborative. As the number of students with special needs continues to increase, the need for more special educators also rises. Given the push to educate students with disabilities in the general education classroom, it is the responsibility of those of us in higher education to make sure that we are preparing special education teachers to successfully serve students with disabilities in inclusive classrooms.

In 1975, Congress passed PL 94-142, the Education for All Handicapped Children Act (now known as the Individuals with Disabilities Education Act [IDEA]), which specified that all children were entitled to a free, appropriate public education (FAPE). In addition, the law specified that special education was to be provided in the least restrictive environment (LRE), which meant that students with disabilities were to be educated to the greatest extent possible in the general education classroom. At the same time, Congress recognized that the general education classroom may not be the most appropriate placement for all students with disabilities and developed a continuum of alternative placements—from part-time resource programs and self-contained classes in regular schools, to separate day and residential treatment facilities. However, educators realize that the intent of IDEA is to include students with disabilities in the general education classroom as much as possible.

Through the implementation of IDEA, educators began using the term *inclusion*, meaning that students with disabilities are served in the general education classroom. However, the term used in IDEA is *continuum of services*, not inclusion. This distinction only adds to the struggle that educators and parents are faced with in defining inclusion. Obviously, there is great variation in the interpretation of this word. For example, some schools set up an inclusion program that includes students with mild to moderate disabilities in the general education classroom while educating students with more significant disabilities in self-contained settings. Other schools support full inclusion, which typically means that all students are educated in the general education setting regardless of the severity of their disability.

One of the major challenges schools are faced with is making sure that teachers are trained to work in an inclusive setting, which is often made up of students with a wide range of levels of academic and behavioral functioning. There has been a great deal of research examining teachers' concerns about inclusion and about the supports that teachers feel are necessary for an effective inclusive classroom. Norrell (1997) found that an effective inclusive classroom requires (a) prior and ongoing training for teachers, (b) additional planning time, (c) limitation on the number of special education students in each general education classroom (no more than three), (d) additional personnel support (e.g., instructional aides), (e) additional monetary resources, and (f) support from principals and other professionals within the building. Teachers are quick to admit that these supports are not always available to them. As a result, some teachers feel ill prepared for the challenge.

Over the past 10 years, we have seen an increase in the number of general education teachers who are returning to higher education to pursue a master's degree in special education. These teachers know that they are going to be teaching students with a wide variety of learning abilities, and they want to be prepared. Fortunately, these teachers benefit greatly from the strategies they learn. In reality, the general education classroom has always included students who varied greatly in their learning abilities, even though some students may not ever have been identified as having special needs. Teachers are able to apply much of what they learn to many students within their classrooms.

Many general education and special education teachers and parents have noted numerous benefits of inclusive education for students with disabilities. Some of these include: (a) increased access to the general education curriculum; (b) more opportunity for peer interactions; (c) peer role models for academic, social, and behavior skills; and (d) increased collaboration between educators. Students without disabilities may also benefit by learning about individual differences, accepting and respecting all people, and increasing their own academic performance by working with their peers.

As a general education teacher, you may be surprised to walk into your classroom and find that you have 24 students including three students who have disabilities—two students with Attention Deficit/Hyperactivity Disorder (ADHD) and one student with autism. Your initial reaction may be that you are completely unprepared to teach in this classroom, when in reality, you have at least had an introduction to special education course in your preservice program and, more than likely, student teaching in an inclusive setting. Now is the time to reach out to your colleagues who have specialized training in special education and begin to develop working relationships with them. They can provide you with general information on disabilities, teaching strategies, behavior management, where to access more training, scheduling, and any other issues that you may need assistance with. Each of these areas is discussed in detail in this book.

As special educators, we have each had the opportunity to work alongside our general education colleagues and are aware of the challenges teachers face on a daily basis. Because of our experiences, we have written this book to provide information to both general education and special education teachers as they come together to ensure the most appropriate education for all students. *Teacher's Survival Guide: The Inclusive Classroom* discusses critical and practical issues and topics for this day and age. This book is comprised of 10 comprehensive and exhaustive chapters addressing important topics first-year inclusive and special education teachers will face. An overview of each chapter follows. Each chapter gives thorough descriptions and explanations of the topics along with many practical examples that first-year teachers should find very beneficial. In addition, each chapter provides the reader with a special section called "Survival Secrets of Teachers," where practicing teachers are interviewed about specific chapter topics. Each chapter also ends with a section called the "Survival Toolkit," which provides the reader with additional websites and resources to further her knowledge base on each specific topic.

Chapter 1, "Professional Expectations," discusses how teachers can collaborate with other school personnel. This includes special and general education teachers, related service personnel, and administrators. It also focuses on school policies and procedures as well as how teachers can better prepare themselves through professional development.

Chapter 2, "Collaboration and Consultation," addresses the benefits of collaboration and barriers to effective collaboration. It also touches upon role clarification and cross-cultural considerations. The ability to work with others is essential for success.

Chapter 3, "Communication With Parents," highlights different communication options and discusses how teachers can handle conflict with parents. Also discussed is the importance of respecting confidentiality and recognizing the impact of a student's disability on the family. Parents are such an important factor in the education of their child, and teachers need to be cognizant of the roles parents play and how to effectively communicate with them.

Chapter 4, "Special Education and the Law," describes the major legislation associated with students with special needs. Legislation addressed includes the Individuals with Disabilities Education Improvement Act, Section 504 of the Rehabilitation Act of 1973, and the Americans with Disabilities Act. After reading this chapter, the reader will have a more comprehensive understanding of these acts, know what is required of him as a teacher, and understand how he will be impacted as a teacher of students with disabilities.

Chapter 5, "Planning Academic Instruction," provides specific information on Individualized Education Programs (IEPs) as well as developing lesson plans. Other topics addressed include instructional strategies and accommodations and modifications. Setting high expectations for all students is also discussed. Lastly, the importance and impact of how the teacher's room is arranged and how classroom rules can impact a student are delineated.

• •

Instructional strategies: Methods, materials, and techniques that can be used to assist students in strengthening their own areas of academic need, thereby enhancing the learning process.

• •

Chapter 6, "Assessment in the Inclusive Classroom," explores the important topic of assessment. This chapter begins by explaining the purposes of assessment and then the difference between formal and informal assessments. It then discusses different types of assessments, including performance-based assessment, portfolios, and self-assessment. Finally, the chapter describes rubrics and how to develop them. It is our hope that this chapter will better prepare you for measuring your students' progress.

Chapter 7, "Classroom Management," discusses how teachers can effectively manage their classrooms. The chapter begins by explaining how teachers can be proactive by incorporating motivation and management techniques. Other options that are explained in detail include classwide positive behavior supports and functional behavioral assessment. Lastly, this chapter talks about how teachers can manage student behavior with success. Managing student behavior is essential for establishing a positive learning environment.

Chapter 8, "Using Data to Support IEP Goals," focuses on the importance of using data to make educational decisions. This chapter dives into the importance of consistent and continuous data use. It discusses how data are used to make decisions and how they can help to identify how a student and teacher are performing. It also addresses how teachers can communicate assessment results to parents and other teachers. As schools move toward more schoolwide programs, data collection and data use will be prominent in making educationally sound and relevant decisions.

Chapter 9, "Technology," touches upon the importance of technology in instruction. It explains what assistive technology is and the different options that exist for students with disabilities. In addition, this chapter highlights factors associated with different operating systems, technology training, and support. Technology is definitely an area that can impact teaching and is constantly changing, so teachers need to be aware of what options they have.

Chapter 10, "Placement Options for Inclusive and Special Education Teachers," addresses different placement options teachers may be considering. We strongly support teachers working in the inclusive classroom setting. However, IDEA does require that schools provide a continuum of services for students with special needs; therefore, there are a number of positions that place teachers in settings that are outside of the general education classroom. The final chapter of this book also provides information on placement options for special education teachers. Although these teaching positions are not as prevalent as they once were, most school districts still hire for these teaching positions.

The text is written in a style that readers can comprehend and is supported with many examples. In addition, the information can be easily applied to all types of teachers in a multitude of different settings. In preparing this book, we wanted to explain and provide a detailed and comprehensive analysis of all of the different topics a teacher in an inclusive classroom must consider when preparing to teach. On the whole, this book will be an added resource to all teachers as they travel on their journey toward a career in education. We are confident that readers will find it helpful and useful regarding all of the aspects associated with teaching in an inclusive classroom.

1 Professional Expectations

When you are hired to teach in an inclusive classroom, you will be expected to know about disability areas, effective teaching practices, adapting and modifying content, assessment, and behavior management, to name a few. In addition, you must be knowledgeable of the professional expectations that go beyond classroom instruction. These professional expectations include (a) collaborative skills in working with other educators, (b) knowledge of policies and school procedures, and (c) professional development. Each of these expectations may include different components depending on your role, but, as an educator, it is vital that you know and understand all aspects of your position.

Collaborating With School Personnel

In order to be a successful inclusive classroom teacher, you need to master the ability to collaborate effectively with school personnel. When you were hired, the school district was confident that you possessed the qualifications, knowledge, skills, and academic preparation to work in an inclusive environment. The idea of inclusion is a relatively new concept, and you will continue to learn about teaching in inclusive settings throughout your teaching career. Each classroom is very different. When there is something you need help with or a question that needs to be answered, your best solution to solving this dilemma might be to ask another teaching professional in the school. This could include

(a) special education teachers, (b) general education teachers, (c) related services personnel, or (d) an administrator.

Special Education and General Education Teachers

Special education teachers are an excellent resource to help field questions, analyze problems, or provide guidance. You might consider setting up a weekly meeting with an experienced special education teacher who has been at your school for a few years to discuss relevant topics (e.g., instruction, student behavior, assessment). Questions you might ask include: "How do you communicate with other teachers?", "What happens if co-teachers are not following the IEP?", and "How do you get parents involved?" Knowing what experienced teachers have found to be successful within the school will assist you in finding out what works best in your new school setting.

If you are a special education teacher in the inclusive classroom, then it will be important to meet with the general education teacher to define and discuss each of your roles and responsibilities. For example, what will your role be? How will you share the teaching responsibilities? Who will do the grading? These types of questions should be answered and agreed upon before the first day of school so that it runs smoothly. Meeting regularly with the general education teacher and having an open line of communication can be an effective strategy to minimize problems. Likewise, if you are a general education teacher in an inclusive classroom, then you will need to do the same thing—meet with the special education teacher and discuss these same issues. Ultimately, the most important part of any classroom is student learning; therefore, it is essential that teachers in inclusive classrooms have these discussions with each other so that they can be as effective as possible.

If a paraeducator is assigned to the classroom, then he or she should also be involved in the definition and discussion of roles and responsibilities. A good idea is to complete a roles and responsibilities chart and to revisit the chart each time student progress reports are completed. This will enable you to compare the roles that each professional has in the classroom with the progress your students are making. If your students are not making sufficient progress, then this may be the time to make some changes. Figure 1 provides a list of some of the topics that need to be discussed prior to the first day of school. This is not an exhaustive list, but it gives you an idea of the issues that need to be discussed. Regardless of the specifics regarding your role, planning in advance is a good way to begin a successful working relationship with your colleagues.

· ·

Paraeducator (or paraprofessional): An adult in the classroom who serves as a teaching assistant and works with children on tasks they are unable to perform on their own.

· ·

Some of the roles and responsibilities that should be discussed include:
- grading papers,
- updating IEP forms,
- collecting homework assignments,
- arranging parent conferences,
- providing assignment and testing accommodations,
- creating assignments and tests,
- taking attendance, and
- handling discipline and discipline referrals.

Figure 1. Roles and responsibilities in the inclusive classroom.

Once everyone's roles and responsibilities are defined, you will have to make some collaborative decisions on the logistics of the classroom. For example, what does a typical day look like? How will you develop your lesson plans? How are all students included? What kinds of materials are accessible for instruction? The general education teacher you are working with would be a good place to start. You need to learn about your teaching environment. We suggest you discuss each other's philosophies on teaching and learning. Get to know the other professionals you are working with, ask them questions, and learn from them. You should also be open to trying new teaching methods and strategies. As a teacher in an inclusive classroom, you need to effectively communicate and work with other teachers to be successful—the end reward will be that all students are learning.

Related Service Personnel

Another group of professionals that you will be collaborating with is related services personnel. This group includes professionals such as the guidance counselor, occupational therapist, physical therapist, social worker, and speech-language pathologist. These individuals can provide critical information that may assist you when working with students with disabilities. Collaborating with these individuals will not only help you in the classroom, but you will also be able to provide them with valuable information they can use when working with your students. In turn, instruction is more consistent, and your students are given more opportunities to work on areas of academic or behavioral needs.

Related services: Services a student with disabilities needs in order to benefit from special education that may include, but are not limited to, speech therapy, physical therapy, and occupational therapy.

Occupational therapist: A professional who works primarily to assist the child with sensory issues and fine motor deficits.

Physical therapist: A professional who focuses on large motor issues, providing information about improving the child's large motor development.

Speech-language pathologist: A professional who treats speech, language, and swallowing disorders.

. . . .

Administrators

Your principal or special education director will be another source for information and guidance. Questions regarding IDEA, the Individualized Education Program (IEP), or any special education service can be directed to individuals in administrative positions. There will be issues that arise that may require you to seek their advice and/or input on issues, and you will want to make sure you have accurate information regarding your students with disabilities. Administrators are charged with ensuring that all legal processes and procedures are followed for all students.

. . . .

Individuals with Disabilities Education Improvement Act (IDEA): This law was initially passed in 1975 as the Education for All Handicapped Children Act and guaranteed that eligible children and youth with disabilities would have a free and appropriate public education (FAPE) available to them, designed to meet their unique educational needs. It was reauthorized and added to in 1990, 1997, and 2004.

Individualized Education Program (IEP): Each public school child who receives special education and related services must have an IEP. Each IEP must be designed for one student and must be an individualized document.

. . . .

School Policies and Procedures

Each school is different and has its own set of policies and procedures that are used to govern the school building. District guidelines must be followed as well. For example, what is the school's code of conduct? Is there a homework policy? Is there a grading policy? Are classroom expectations explained to teachers and students? When a student misbehaves, are there school-level consequences? Students and parents need to know that you are knowledgeable regarding these policies and procedures and can implement them in a consistent manner. As a teacher in an inclusive classroom, you have a lot to learn and you might make mistakes, but if you act professionally and analyze the data in a given situation before making a decision, then you will earn students' and parents' respect and trust over time.

Learning the policies and procedures of your school is important, but it will take some time. Most schools will provide pertinent information in two ways. They may have a website that will provide some basic information about the school's policies and procedures, and they will probably have a handbook of information for teachers and other professionals in the building. In addition, there is typically an orientation session for new teachers that will cover many of the policies and procedures that you may need to know prior to the first day of school. Do not hesitate to ask questions. Use the resources provided and review the information often so that you can be consistent and make meaningful and accurate decisions.

Professional Development

As a teacher in an inclusive classroom, you will bring all of the knowledge that you have gained in your teacher education program to the classroom and the school; however, learning does not end on the day of your college graduation. In many ways it is just beginning. Continued professional development is essential in helping teachers continue learning, developing, and refining their teaching skills. Professional development is typically offered as an in-service training or an educational conference. These trainings can have a student-, teacher-, or school-related focus or may address issues related to parents and the community. Professional development is important because it allows teachers the opportunity to improve themselves and become better teachers. When considering professional development opportunities, consider session length, the expertise of the presenter, content, and outcomes. As with any opportunity, some are worth the money and others are not, so make sure to do your research prior to making a commitment to attend.

Inclusive classroom: Classroom that includes all children, both with and without disabilities.

Some opportunities, such as teacher in-services that are provided by your school, may be mandatory; however, there are many educational trainings and conferences presented throughout the year. When considering what would be the most beneficial professional development training, conducting a self-assessment to identify your strengths and challenges as a teacher and the location of the professional development opportunities will help in the decision-making process.

Self-Assessment

All teachers need to regularly conduct a self-assessment of their knowledge and skills with regard to being an effective teacher. You will continue to learn from other educators in your school, and possibly through connections you made as a college student, but much of your continued professional development will need to consist of purposeful opportunities. Teachers need to be proactive and seek out and find opportunities/experiences to further their teaching skills. By conducting a self-assessment of your own teaching skills, you will be able to clearly see what areas you need to address. See Table 1 for a sample self-assessment conducted by a new teacher.

Taking the time to analyze what areas you are proficient in and what areas you need to learn more about will help you make better choices regarding professional development opportunities. Given that many of these trainings and conferences charge a fee, it is best to create a priority list of topics to follow before attending.

Strengths/Challenges

After conducting a self-assessment, you should be able to highlight your teaching strengths as well as your challenges. This information can be very revealing and advantageous. You can use this information to help other teachers and to seek out help for yourself. Many schools have an internal professional development system, meaning that teachers in a school provide professional development to each other to help them develop their knowledge and skills. All teachers should be prepared to provide professional development to their colleagues. Not only can you provide knowledge and skills to others, but you can also develop positive working relationships with others by providing continued support. When individuals want to ask you questions or possibly implement your ideas into their classrooms, being available shows support for your colleagues and your school. Likewise, by attending these trainings, you can garner knowledge and ideas from other educators as well as other resources in your school.

Professional development: Informal or formal learning experience that is designed to improve your skills as an educator.

Seeking Out Opportunities

As a teacher, it is often your responsibility to seek out professional development opportunities. As noted earlier, there are many of these educational

Table 1
Sample Self-Assessment of Knowledge and Skills

Content/Skills I Know	Content/Skills I Need More Knowledge About
• Characteristics of students with disabilities • Effective instruction • Lesson planning • Curriculum development • Behavior management • Data-based instruction • Adaptations/modifications • Instructional technology • Assessment • Functional behavioral assessment • Collaboration	• Response to Intervention • Positive behavior supports • Differentiated instruction • Assistive technology • Transition

opportunities offered throughout the year. They can be found locally, regionally/statewide, or nationally/internationally. There are advantages and disadvantages to each of these professional development opportunities.

Local. The school district, a neighboring school district, a community college, a professional organization, an agency, or a university may sponsor local professional development opportunities. Speakers could also be local, or they could be educators who were specifically hired to provide the training. These opportunities may be free or cost a small amount, but minimal travel is involved and you will not have to pay for any type of housing. These events are excellent opportunities for teams of teachers from your school to attend and learn together. Often, schools will send a few teachers to professional development training and then have them present the information to other teachers in their school. Administrators typically embrace this model because the cost is minimal.

Regional/State. Another professional development activity serves a broader spectrum and has either a regional or state presence. These trainings/conferences may be sponsored by the same entities as a local professional development activity, but often they are connected to an educational organization or a university. These opportunities are developed to attract teachers from a certain area or region of a state. They may last more than one day, which might require an overnight stay. Along with a fee for attending this type of professional development activity (which can get costly), the training is more comprehensive and provides attendees with additional materials and resources. Attendees can also make connections with other teachers in the state and may even develop collaborative partnerships. Because of the cost, administrators may only be willing to send one or two teachers. If administrators are not willing to pay for a conference, then they may be willing to provide professional development leave even though the expenses would have to be paid by the attendee. This model has proven to be effective, but because there are fewer attendees from each school at the event, teachers must pay close attention so that they may effectively communicate the information to their colleagues back at school.

National/International. The last professional development activity serves an even broader spectrum and has a national or international presence. These trainings/conferences could be sponsored by the same entities as noted above and are often connected to a professional organization or university. These opportunities are developed to attract teachers from throughout the nation and world. Attending these types of conferences can be costly, but you will have the opportunity to hear experts from around the globe, network with a wide range of professionals, and gather numerous materials and resources for your school. This is an excellent opportunity to not only extend your current teaching skills, but also learn the most current research and updates on the federal regulations for special education.

◇◇◇

SURVIVAL SECRETS OF TEACHERS

Jeff, High School Special Education Teacher

What Is Your Current Position and How Long Have You Been Teaching?

Currently, I am teaching high school students (grades 9–12). I have been teaching for 5 years in inclusive classrooms, resource rooms, and self-contained classrooms.

What Were Some of the Issues You Faced Regarding Professional Expectations as a First-Year Teacher?

My first year of teaching I felt very alone and lost. Not only did I have a new job, but I also was in a brand-new environment where most of the other teachers had been for years. I was very unsure of what I was supposed to do, how I was supposed to act, and what the rules and policies were. Luckily, a veteran teacher took me under her wing and helped guide me to be the teacher I am today. I was so focused on being a good teacher for my students that I got lost in everything else. In college you learn how to be an efficient and effective teacher, but rarely do you learn how to assimilate into a school. Yes, I had an opportunity to student teach, but that was different. For student teaching, there were set guidelines and expectations. As a first-year teacher you are on your own, making your own decisions, teaching your own students, and impacting others with your behavior. It wasn't hard to be professional, but learning to work with all of the different key personnel in the school was a challenge. Again, I wasn't a student anymore, but a real teacher with responsibilities. Over time, I did start to learn more and more about the school policies and procedures and school personnel. Just remember that it will take time to assimilate into your school, but in most cases, there are other people wanting to help you. Also, the school administrators wouldn't have hired you if they didn't think you would be successful.

How Did You Familiarize Yourself With Your School and District?

In order to learn about my school and district, I did a number of things. First, I read the high school student hand-book. I looked at all of the rules and procedures and tried to familiarize myself with all of the school policies. Next, I asked other teachers. I asked teachers to explain any areas I was unclear about. I also asked them about policies on grading, teacher absences, professional development days, and discipline procedures. The last thing I did was go to the district website. I perused this site to learn about the district and then I went to my school site to learn all about my school. I was able to find the names of teachers I would be working with, the vision and mission of the district and school, state assessment data, and more about the culture of the district and school. I was able to find out sports that were offered, clubs, musical and theatrical opportunities, academic opportunities, and many other things that I would not have known had I not checked these sites.

What Advice Would You Give Future Teachers About Professional Expectations?

Learn all you can about your school and district. Be proactive and seek out the knowledge you desire. Be observant. As you go through the school day, notice what happens, who does what, and how things are handled. You would be surprised at how much you can learn just by watching what goes on. There is no way you could possibly learn everything about how a school and district operate. Ask questions. Don't be afraid of how you will look if you ask the wrong question. In my opinion, there is no wrong question. The only wrong question is the one that is never asked. Lastly, remember that you are a teacher and a role model. Students, teachers, and administrators are constantly observing how you act and behave and interact with others. Behave appropriately and always think before you act.

◇◇◇

Conclusion

Obtaining a teaching position in a good school district is exciting and encouraging—all of your time in college has finally paid off. However, teaching is only a portion of your new job. All teachers must be aware of the professional expectations that come with their profession. First, teachers need to be able to collaborate and effectively work with other school personnel (this holds especially true in an inclusive classroom). Communication is key. Next, teachers need to be aware of school policies and procedures. All school personnel need to learn about the characteristics of their school, how the school functions from the administrative office down to the classroom, and how they fit into the big scheme of things.

Finally, teachers have to be able to assess their own knowledge and skills and seek out opportunities to improve these. Teaching is a profession that is constantly changing and evolving. In order to keep up with the changes and be as effective as possible, general or special education teachers in inclusive classrooms need to be cognizant of professional expectations and how important they are to students, parents, and other school personnel.

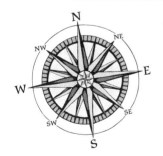

Survival Tips

- Take advantage of in-service opportunities that will help you expand your knowledge in teaching students with a wide range of levels of academic and behavioral functioning.

- Be proactive in asking for help from your colleagues.

- As a professional, you need to know the district and school policies and procedures.

Survival Toolkit

Websites to Support You With Professionalism

- The Role of Teacher Professionalism in Education: http://students. ed.uiuc.edu/vallicel/Teacher_Professionalism.html

- Guide to First Year Teaching/Legal stuff you need to know/Ethics and professional expectations: http://en.wikibooks.org/wiki/ Guide_to_First_Year_Teaching/Legal_stuff_you_need_to_know/ Ethics_and_professional_expectations

- Great Expectations: Good News for Beginning Teachers: http:// www.janebluestein.com/articles/great_exps.html

- Association of American Educators: Code of Ethics: http://www. aaeteachers.org/index.php/about-us/aae-code-of-ethics

- Teachers' (Code of Ethics): http://www.education.gov.mt/ministry/ doc/code_of_ethics.htm

- National Education Association: Code of Ethics: http://www.nea. org/aboutnea/code.html

Books to Support You With Professionalism

Carr, D. (2000). *Professionalism and ethics in teaching*. London, England: Routledge.

Gill, V. (2005). *The ten commandments of professionalism for teachers: Wisdom from a veteran teacher*. Thousand Oaks, CA: Corwin Press.

Hurst, B., & Reding, G. (2008). *Professionalism in teaching* (2nd ed.). Boston, MA: Prentice Hall.

2 Collaboration and Consultation

Collaboration is a school philosophy and teacher practice that falls under many different names (Leatherman, 2009). It has been applied to school-based professional development practices, including staff development and curriculum planning, and to school-based service configurations such as multidisciplinary teams, teaming, and co-teaching (Villa, Thousand, Nevin, & Malgeri, 1996). There are a couple of broad collaboration definitions that are widely accepted by the education community. Cook and Friend (1993) defined collaboration as a style of direct interaction between at least two equal parties voluntarily engaging in shared decision making as they work toward a common goal. Idol, Nevin, and Paolucci-Whitcomb (1994) defined collaboration as an interactive process that enables people with diverse expertise to generate creative solutions to mutually defined problems. Both definitions are broad and encompass many important aspects that are not necessarily written into the definition. Cook and Friend (1993) identified seven characteristics to further clarify their definition. Those characteristics include interchanges that are (a) voluntary, (b) based on parity, (c) share a common goal, (d) include shared decision making, (e) are accountable for outcomes, (f) are based on shared resources, and (g) have emerging trust and respect. At the core of the two definitions lie at least two people with mutual respect and interest working together to solve problems and working toward common goals.

Often, collaborative efforts involve an aspect of consultation. In most work environments, consultation is an expert-driven model in which someone with extensive knowledge in a certain content area is paired with a teacher or other professional. Teachers who have a consultative coaching relationship—that is, who share aspects of teaching, have effective means of communication, pool their experiences, and plan together—practice and implement new skills and strategies and apply them more appropriately (Joyce & Showers, 2002).

A consultative coach models the qualities of a skilled facilitator. Coaches have both instructional and content expertise and promote and support high-quality instruction through direct, school-based work with other teachers and professionals. Coaches observe classroom instruction, model lessons, and coach teachers one-on-one or in small groups. The coach role combines the skills of active listening and strong facilitation to help create an environment that impacts teaching and learning. Consultative coaches are a part of the collaborative team and are present at team meetings for brainstorming, collaborative learning, and problem solving.

Benefits of Collaboration

Benefits to Students

Students, professionals, and parents benefit when schools adopt the philosophy and practices of a collaborative educational environment. Students with and without disabilities agree that when general and special education teachers collaborate to provide instruction there is a deeper understanding of material, a rise in self-esteem, a more positive effect on grades, and an increase in the amount of teacher help they receive (Gerber & Popp, 1999). Likewise, Spraker (2003) reported that there was a positive correlation between teacher collaboration and grade point averages of students in the collaborative educational environment. The results were derived from studies investigating the impact of collaboration on both general and special education students. When general and special educators collaborate to teach students, the students receive the benefit of instruction and intervention planned by two teachers (Cook & Friend, 1993).

One of the biggest benefits of collaboration for individuals with disabilities is that the stigma of a specific disability is reduced (Cook & Friend, 1993). When the barrier between general and special educators is eliminated, many of the barriers between students are also removed. Children with disabilities no longer stand out in the crowd as they enter and exit the general education classroom. In fact, they become members of the classroom—not just visitors. However, the general and special educator need to work together to make sure that the student with a disability is not identified or singled out in the general education classroom.

Lastly, when collaboration is valued and practiced in schools, teacher referrals decrease as does the number of students eligible for special education services (Cook & Friend, 1993). This is especially important in schools with a focus on Response to Intervention (RtI). The focus of the collaborative team is to support the child, and there is a sense of ownership shared by everyone. There is no longer a need to remove a child from one system and place her into another. She will remain in a unified system, and even though the intensity of support may increase, the environment will not change.

Benefits to Teachers and Other Professionals

Researchers have found that collaborative teaming improves the overall school climate for teachers and increases their feelings of effectiveness (Spraker, 2003). The concept itself promotes socialization with and learning from other professionals. This process helps to diminish the sense of isolation a teacher may feel when she is secluded within her classroom for the better part of a day. This is especially important for teachers in inclusive classrooms. When teachers are connected in the education community, there are higher rates of job satisfaction and teacher retention reported (Cook & Friend, 1993).

Most importantly, because the barrier between general and special education is removed, communication is increased and everyone's roles and responsibilities are valued (Cook & Friend, 1993). This removes the doubt and frustration on both sides. For instance, the general educator no longer feels that he does all of the planning while the special education teacher just floats around the school. The opposite would also be a good example. The special education teacher no longer feels she is doing all of the work modifying or adapting lessons while the general education teacher just does minimal planning.

Barriers to Effective Collaboration

Anytime there are benefits, there are also typically barriers. Barriers will exist in a school until it, as a whole, recognizes the barriers and addresses them. The primary barrier to teacher collaboration is time (Conderman & Johnston-Rodriguez, 2009; Cook & Friend, 1993; Worrell, 2008). For teachers to be successful working together, collaboration should occur face-to-face on a weekly basis. This type of schedule can be difficult to uphold given scheduling conflicts and the nature of the traditional school structure, but teachers need to try to meet consistently and often for their own benefit and that of their students.

Another barrier is inadequate teacher preparation. In most cases, general education teachers are exposed to only one course on the characteristics associated with different disabilities. This does not provide preservice teachers enough information or the necessary skills to be competent in collaboration. Even though they may feel like they are good collaborators, ongoing professional collaboration requires teachers to have sophisticated skills in the areas of conflict resolution and communication. Other important skills include how to listen, how to manage resistance, and how to run efficient meetings (Cook & Friend, 1993).

Building a Collaborative Team

Building a collaborative team is not an easy process. Teachers will need to work very hard at establishing an effective and efficient collaborative team. Villa et al. (1996) identified six elements of collaboration. They asserted that members (a) agree that every stakeholder possesses unique and needed expertise, (b) emphasize task completion and relationship building, (c) distribute leadership roles and hold other members accountable, (d) engage in frequent face-to-face contact, (e) understand the importance of reciprocity, and (f) agree to consciously practice and increase their social interaction opportunities.

Gerber and Popp (1999) communicated the importance of how administrators and education staff develop a districtwide and schoolwide policy that makes a commitment to inclusive practices and collaboration. This policy must be communicated with all stakeholders including the parents of children with and without disabilities. Everyone involved should understand what exactly is happening in the classroom and school. In effect, collaboration should be part of a code of ethics and an integral part of the culture of the school (Cook & Friend, 1993). Education of all children should also be included in the district and school's mission statements. Special attention should be paid to ensuring that teachers and other personnel have ownership in the ethics and culture of collaboration, which means that teachers need to be a part of the initial decision-making process and the development of these schoolwide policies.

Collaboration doesn't just happen in a school or district. For effective collaboration to occur, administrators need to provide their staff with adequate time for planning activities and evaluating progress toward their goals (Gerber & Popp, 1999; Leatherman, 2009). At a minimum, weekly—but optimally, daily—planning meetings are vital in order for all collaborative teams to run efficiently and effectively. This means that administrators need to schedule teachers' open periods at the same time during the school day so that they can meet with each other.

Several researchers discussed the importance of providing professional development opportunities (Cook & Friend, 1993; Gerber & Popp, 1999). Training should focus on running efficient meetings, effective communication skills, and conflict resolution strategies. Teachers are more likely to collaborate if they receive support and ongoing training about the collaborative process (Spraker, 2003). Ensuring that general and special education teachers have an opportunity to participate in collaboration training together (Villa et al., 1996) will only serve to encourage relationships between the team members.

Effective collaborative teams identify the roles and responsibilities of their members (Cook & Friend, 1993). In the beginning of this process, the teachers should sit down and talk with each other about their roles and responsibilities and figure out what each person will do, how they will work together, and each person's areas of strength. This incorporates a feeling of shared contribution by all team members. People should not feel like visitors or unequal partners (Leatherman, 2009). In addition, team procedures should be respected and adhered to in order to promote efficacy and accountability. Teachers should plan to meet and revisit these roles and responsibilities to make sure they are on track and happy with their progress. If things are not going well in the classroom, then changes can be made. Another characteristic of collaborative teams is setting clear team goals (Cook & Friend, 1993) that should be understood and supported by each member of the team (Worrell, 2008). Lastly, administrative support is needed for the collaborative process to be successful (Leatherman, 2009).

Team Building

Teams are described by Friend and Cook (2007) as two or more individuals who come together to work collaboratively to achieve an agreed-upon common goal. Direct communication, coordination, and clear procedures are other factors necessary for effective teams. The successful foundation of these teams and how they will effectively and efficiently work are built on trust between the general and special education teacher. Consequently, it is generally worth the extra time invested for team building, particularly when participants will be working together over an extended time period (e.g., more than a few weeks). The purpose of team building is to create rapport and trust, to let participants get acquainted, and to establish more comfortable working relationships. Introductions of participants and their roles are a simple but effective starting point. This may begin with small groups of two members who chat together briefly, then introduce one another to the entire group. Other partner or team activities such as puzzles, problem-solving scenarios, or ice-breaking activities are widely available. Many ice-breaking activities can be created from just using participants' biographical information. A list of descriptors (e.g., likes pizza, has 3 cousins) can be created on a page, each followed by a blank. Participants can be instructed to mingle to see how many items they can complete in a specified time period, using each individual's name only once. More extensive team-building exercises for the workplace can be located with a quick Internet search.

Role Clarification

Team membership needs to be flexible, modifiable, and complimentary to represent the range of services needed for each individual case, bringing a wide range of expertise and experience to the table. For the most effective teams possible, team members should be added and subtracted as issues are resolved or additional needs arise. As new teams are established, it is helpful for team members to explain their roles as well as their responsibilities and how they can benefit the team, particularly when family members are included on the team.

Cross-Cultural Considerations

Cross-cultural communication adds another important variable for team effectiveness. Therefore, it is essential that team members are sensitive to cross-cultural beliefs, perspectives, communication patterns, and interactions (Jairrels, 1999). For example, different cultures may have unique family structures as well as differing beliefs about child rearing, the nature and cause of disabilities, the family-school relationship, and the purpose of schools. Team members must be aware of their own perspectives and beliefs and sensitive to the cultures of others. This will help them to avoid the common pitfalls related to cross-cultural interactions such as stereotyping or assuming that all members of a particular group have identical values and beliefs.

Various cultures have their own rules regarding turn taking as well as other verbal and nonverbal rules of conversation. For example, eye contact, personal space, touch, proximity, and the use of gestures have different meanings in different cultures (Salend, 2005). Teachers must also remember that paraprofessionals and community members may be valuable resources for interpreting behaviors and interactions in a social and cultural context. When educators and families speak different languages, interpreters who speak the same dialect should be included in the conversations. Salend (2005), however, strongly advised against using children or other students as interpreters. This can cause awkward moments and a child should not be put into this kind of situation.

SURVIVAL SECRETS OF TEACHERS

John, Middle School Special Education Teacher

What Is Your Current Position and How Long Have You Been Teaching?

I am currently teaching in a middle school that is comprised of students in the seventh and eighth grades. Currently, most of my teaching occurs in a resource room, but I also teach in some inclusive classes. I have been teaching for 4 years.

What Are Some Challenges You Faced in Collaborating With Other Teachers as a First-Year Teacher?

As a first-year teacher, it was initially very difficult for me to collaborate. It took some time to get myself situated in my new role as a special education teacher and really figure out how the school functioned. I also spent a lot of time learning about the specific needs of my students. Given that I was spending so much time on these issues, I did not do much with the actual teachers in my building. What I mean is that I did not really try to establish relationships with other teachers. I guess you could say I was just trying to survive and meet the needs of my students. Little did I know how important it was to collaborate with other teachers who also worked with my students. The biggest challenge was to approach teachers after the school year had already begun and to try to communicate with them. After the school year started, other teachers became extremely busy taking care of their own content and planning for their instruction. It was also difficult to find a common time with many teachers to discuss the needs of my students.

What Strategies Did You Employ to Collaborate With Other Teachers?

One thing I learned after my first year was to communicate with other teachers early and often. During my second year, I communicated with teachers prior to the beginning of the school year. Prior to the start of the school year, we had some in-service training days, and I set up meetings with teachers to discuss my students and their needs. I offered teachers suggestions, and I also fielded their questions. This helped to establish a positive rapport, and future meetings and discussions were then much easier to schedule. I also learned that everyone is busy, so I figured out times that were convenient for the other teachers to meet. The last thing I did was to make up little note cards for each of my students to give to the other teachers. On the card it listed the student's name, his strength areas, the areas he had difficulties with, modifications that needed to be made for his optimal learning, and possible strategies teachers could implement in their classes.

What Changes Have You Made Since Your First Year in Terms of Collaboration?

The biggest change I have made is to be openly available and proactive. I do not wait until there is a problem, but I work with teachers whenever I can. I send notes, talk with them, help them plan lessons, field their questions, and offer support. In many cases, some of the teachers have little experience working with students with disabilities, so I make myself available whenever they ask. I have also led some small in-services in our school about students with disabilities to help educate all of the other teachers. These in-services have been well received and now teachers understand my role better and what we need to do together to meet the needs of these students.

Conclusion

As schools move more and more to including students with special needs in the general education classroom, it is imperative that teachers learn to collaborate and have the ability to function and work with others. General education teachers typically have limited knowledge of special education and the students who are served. Remember, this limited knowledge is primarily due to the constant changes in special education law and the innovative technologies being introduced to the field. This means that teachers will need to learn from professional development and other teachers and administrators with more experience or backgrounds. In many cases, if you are a special education teacher in an inclusive setting, then you may be designated as the resource to help support the general education teacher. If you are a general education teacher in the inclusion classroom, then you may be perceived as the content expert, but not the expert on inclusion. It really depends on your experience working in inclusive classrooms. Regardless of your actual role in the inclusion setting, you will need to be able to collaborate and work with your colleagues as you are learning new information to better serve the students in the classroom. Knowing how to effectively collaborate will be very important for your success and the success of your students.

In addition, understanding cooperative teaching, what it entails, and how to effectively communicate with other teachers in these situations are critical elements of which you should be aware. A large part of your success will come from your interpersonal skills. You need to know how to effectively communicate with others and be cognizant of your own strengths and weaknesses in order to become a better communicator. These skills will serve you well when you are faced with difficult colleagues. Lastly, you may want to investigate the possibility of working with a mentor who can provide guidance as you are learning your new teaching position. You do not have to feel alone. The ability to collaborate and communicate effectively will not only make your job easier and more exciting, but it will also assist you on your journey to becoming a master teacher.

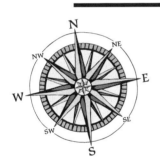

Survival Tips

- General and special education teachers who take the time to plan together can more easily define their roles and responsibilities.

- Collaboration is more effective when all stakeholders are willing to work together.

- Develop a system for dealing with disagreements among colleagues.

Survival Toolkit

Websites to Support You With Collaboration

- Collaboration Skills: http://www.learningforward.org/standards/collaborationskills.cfm

- Collaboration and Consultation: http://www.circleofinclusion.org/english/pim/four/coll.html

- Making Collaboration and Consultation Work: http://www.circleofinclusion.org/english/pim/four/work.html

- Collaborative Teaching–Special Education in Collaborative Classrooms: http://learningdisabilities.about.com/od/publicschoolprograms/p/collaboration.htm
- Schools and Special Education: http://cecp.air.org/schools_special.asp

Books to Support You With Collaboration

Dettmer, P., Thurston, L. P., Knackendoffel, A., & Dyck, N. J. (2005). *Collaboration, consultation, and teamwork for students with special needs* (6th ed.). Boston, MA: Allyn & Bacon.

Simpson, C. G., & Bakken, J. P. (2011). *Collaboration: A multidisciplinary approach to educating students with disabilities.* Waco, TX: Prufrock Press.

3 Communicating With Parents

With all that goes into being a good inclusive classroom teacher, one must not forget that an important characteristic of successful teachers is the ability to have effective and ongoing communication with parents of students with disabilities. Inclusion teachers need to be extremely cognizant of parents' needs in relation to their child. It is important to keep parents "in the loop" with regard to their child's progress and allow them the opportunity to give input on what happens with their child's home and school activities. Knowing how to develop a system for parental communications, handle conflict with parents, respect confidentiality, and recognize the needs of siblings and the impact of a disability on a family are all important aspects of developing healthy relationships with parents.

In an inclusive classroom environment, teachers must face the reality that not all families will understand the value of an inclusive classroom. It is possible that parents may raise concern over safety issues or question if academic progress is hindered in this type of environment. "In helping families to understand the inclusive classroom, remain open and honest about the outcomes and challenges that children will experience" (Simpson & Warner, 2010, pg. 197). All forms of communication with parents should be based on this principle.

Parent Communications

Both general and special education teachers need to be able to effectively communicate with parents. It is important to note that communication can have a positive or a negative focus. In other words, do you only communicate with parents when there are problems with their children? Call parents the first week or two of school to introduce yourself, discuss your role in educating their child, and identify the most effective way for them to contact you. This is also a good time to get additional input about their child regarding previously effective classroom strategies or any other information they would like to share about their child. It is important to make the very first contact with the parents a positive one. By doing so, you have begun to establish an effective communication link with the parents, and if you have to deal with a particularly challenging subject, then the parents will be more apt to work with you in the future.

It is also important to consistently communicate with parents throughout the year. Parents need to know that they can contact you when they have questions or concerns. As part of your record keeping, it will be important to document communication with parents. You will want to keep a log of communications made to parents that include the date, the type of contact, what was discussed, and the outcome. Having documentation you can refer to later can be very important if parents file complaints or in case of discrepancies. Teachers may choose to communicate with parents via:

- face-to-face interaction,
- phone calls,
- written communication,
- e-mail communication, or
- a combination of communication techniques.

See Figure 2 for a sample of a parent communication log.

Teachers should also be aware of the language they use with parents. Be professional and clarify any information that may be confusing or misinterpreted. Consider that variation in parents' background knowledge, socioeconomic status, and culture may impact your communication style.

Face-to-Face Interactions

Face-to-face interactions could consist of a more formal parent-teacher conference where specific information is discussed, such as academic progress and social behavior, or of an informal meeting before or after school when a parent is picking up his child. In face-to-face interactions, it is important that you pay special attention to the parents by making eye contact and listening. It can be discouraging to parents when a teacher looks like she is in a hurry to be

Date:	Details of Communication:
Student Name:	
Parent Name:	
Type of Communication:	
Time:	
Date:	Details of Communication:
Student Name:	
Parent Name:	
Type of Communication:	
Time:	
Date:	Details of Communication:
Student Name:	
Parent Name:	
Type of Communication:	
Time:	

Figure 2. Parent communication log.

somewhere else. Parents need to know that their concerns are validated. You will be making a lasting impression on the parents, so make sure it is a positive one. Table 2 will help you in interpreting nonverbal gestures you may receive from parents during face-to-face interactions. It is important to recognize that sometimes how something is said has greater meaning than what is being said. For example, a parent may say that he feels comfortable with a decision. However, if this is said while the individual is wringing his hands or his lip is quivering, then he may actually be feeling anxious about the decision, and a discussion on the topic should continue until he is more comfortable and accepting of the decision.

Table 2
Nonverbal Gestures and Their Meanings

Openness, Confidence:
- open hands, palms up
- eye contact
- smile, leaning forward, relaxed
- standing straight, feet slightly apart, shoulders squared

Cooperation, Readiness:
- a person moves closer to another
- open arms or hands (palms out)
- smile
- eye contact

Indifference, Boredom:
- leg over arm of chair
- rhythmic drumming, tapping
- glancing at exit
- yawning
- fidgeting or rocking

Evaluation, Interest:
- leaning forward (positive) and leaning back (negative)
- head tilted
- sucking on tip of pencil or earpiece of glasses indicates wish for nourishment in form of more information
- arched eyebrows

Self-Control, Inner Conflict:
- hand holding wrist or arm
- suppressed gestures or displacement activities such as fist clenched and hidden in pocket
- hand to mouth in astonishment or fear (suppressed scream)
- blowing nose and coughing (disguised tears)

Doubt:
- pacing
- eyes closed
- brow furrowed
- frown

Suspicion, Secretiveness:
- folded arms
- moving away from another
- lack of eye contact
- frown
- scrunching in with head down
- throat clearing

Need for Reassurance:
- clenched hands with thumbs rubbing
- stroking arms
- cuticle picking
- sucking on pen, glasses, etc.

Anxiety:
- nail biting
- sighing
- hand wringing
- rapid, twitchy movements
- lips quivering
- chewing on things

Frustration, Anger:
- making fists
- hands on hips
- stomping
- lips pressed together, jaw muscles tight
- clenched hands with white knuckles
- hostile stare

Defensiveness:
- hands in pocket
- clenched hands
- folded arms (can be reinforced by making fists)
- body twisted away, moving away, sitting back
- looking at door

Dominating:
- elevating self, like standing when others are sitting
- taking a different posture than others in a group, especially hands behind head
- loud voice or low voice carefully enunciated
- standing or walking with hands behind back and chin up

Superior, Subordinate:
- can violate the subordinate's space, and can express doubt, evaluation, domineering gestures
- more likely to signify self-control, anxiety, defensiveness gesture clusters
- putting feet on desk

Professional:
- taking notes
- leaning forward
- eye contact
- index finger to lip to restrain from interrupting

From *Special Needs Advocacy Resource Book* by R. Weinfeld and M. Davis, 2008, p. 256, Waco, TX: Prufrock Press. Copyright 2008 Prufrock Press. Reprinted with permission.

Phone Calls

A simple phone call may solve an issue quickly. Given people's busy schedules, a phone call may also provide access to parents when it is convenient for them. Take notes during the phone call so you can follow up in writing or via e-mail to verify the information that was discussed. Make sure the information is accurate. As previously mentioned, it is important to document all forms of parent communication, including phone conversations.

Written Communication

Written communication can take the form of letters, notes, or newsletters. A newsletter will include information that pertains to all of the students in the class, and it is a good way to keep parents informed of class activities. Some schools develop schoolwide newsletters, while others prefer for teachers to create their own classroom newsletter. If you are expected to create a newsletter, then be sure that it contains timely information and encourages families to become more involved in the classroom. Items that can be included in the newsletter are:

- content about what children are learning while they are in school;
- books or activities that can be read at home to supplement school work;
- monthly or weekly event calendars;
- information from the school nurse such as upcoming health screenings (e.g., vision, hearing) or recent contagious diseases such as chicken pox or pink eye outbreaks;
- website information to access tutorials for schoolwork;
- requests for family members to assist with in-school and out-of-school events (i.e., field trips, art events, science fairs);
- reminders on school forms that are due (e.g., vaccine reminders, permission to participate forms); and
- updates about recent activities that have taken place at school. This can include photos of events or projects that children have worked on.

The actual format of the newsletter you use will depend on your particular preferences. However, remember that literacy levels vary among families, and it is important to use clear language that does not include higher level vocabulary that may prove difficult for families who have English as a second language or those with little or no educational background. Software and templates are available that will help guide you in determining the best format for your newsletter. For example, Microsoft Word offers a variety of newsletter templates that allow you to insert your own information. These can be found at http://office.microsoft.com/en-us/templates/CT010104328.aspx.

Although newsletters are an excellent way to share information with the families of your students, a letter or note is sometimes warranted. Letters and/ or notes are more personal than a newsletter, and parents may appreciate that you took the time to write directly to them. The use of letters and notes is a good way to keep up positive communications. Depending on the child, you may want to mail this information to the parents. Not all students are able to transport a letter home. If you suspect that this may be the case, another option would be to physically hand parents the written communication. As with newsletters, the format of the letter will vary depending on your preference and what type of letter or note you are writing. For instance, a formal letter is used when addressing an issue where the documentation of communication is needed, such as a letter that provides an update on a student's disciplinary action or participation in a specific event. However, you would not want to use a formal or businesslike letter when sending a thank you or a quick daily update on a student's successes. Regardless of the format or type of letter you are sending out, it is important to remember to:

- use proper grammar,
- use correct sentence structure,
- correctly spell words,
- correctly spell the child's and parents' names,
- proofread your letter before sending it out,
- always show respect for the family and the culture of the family in your language and the content you send,
- be clear and to the point, and
- keep a copy of this communication if it is important for documentation.

E-Mail Communication

Many schools and teachers are now including e-mail account information on their school websites as another way for parents to contact teachers. In addition, when parents register their child the first day of classes, they often are being asked to supply their e-mail information to the school and teachers. Through e-mail, teachers can send updates, prompts, notices, and any other pertinent information directly to parents. Parents can receive class e-mails that are intended for all parents or individual e-mails specifically addressing their child. This is a very quick and efficient way to communicate to parents. It is important to note that all families will not necessarily have access to e-mail. In addition to e-mail, there should also be another form of communication implemented.

Teachers should also carefully edit and proofread any e-mails before sending them. It is never a good idea to send something you want parents to read and understand when there are mistakes in it. We also like to point out that e-mail, as with all kinds of written communication, can be interpreted by the receiver in different ways. If you use e-mail correspondence, then you should read up on e-mail etiquette to be sure that you are communicating in the most effective way possible.

You also need to be careful when using e-mail with parents. Make sure this is their preferred way to correspond, and be careful how often you send e-mails. Too many e-mails might actually turn into a hindrance to parents, leading them to refrain from reading the mail. We suggest you find a good time (like every Friday) to send the e-mail so parents know when to expect it. This e-mail could be in the form of an update of what was done the previous week and a look into what will be happening in the future.

When sending e-mails, make sure that the e-mail address is correct and that the e-mail states what you intended it to say. In other words, proofread your e-mail very carefully, as this is a reflection of you as a teacher, and you do not want to send inaccurate or incorrect information to parents. With regard to confidentiality, you might also think about blind carbon copying e-mail addresses so parents don't accidentally receive the other parents' addresses. Good information about e-mail etiquette can be found at http//www.letterwritingguide.com/emailetiquette.htm.

Combination of Communication Techniques

Probably the most effective and efficient way to communicate with parents is to incorporate multiple methods of communication into your teaching practices. This may be different for each set of parents, but implementing more than one type of communication will ensure that parents are receiving accurate and up-to-date information.

Handling Conflict With Parents

When working with parents, you may incur obstacles or times when your actions or the actions of others do not meet the parents' expectations. More directly, there may be times where some type of problem or conflict exists. When a problem or conflict does occur, it needs to be addressed as soon as possible. As an inclusion teacher, you do not want to ignore the conflict by thinking it will go away. Often, ignoring a situation sends the message that you do not care, and this may make the situation worse. In order to address the problem or conflict, it will be necessary to follow these suggested steps:

- identify the problem,
- get the parent's viewpoint,
- identify and discuss possible solutions, and
- reach a consensus that most benefits the student.

Each of the steps listed above will be described in more detail in the following sections.

Identifying the Problem

The first step when dealing with any type of problem or conflict is to identify the problem. Is the problem related directly to the parent or is it student related? Is the problem happening throughout the day or only during a specific time of the day? What is the specific child's problem from the parent's perspective? Identifying the actual problem is very important in order to try to resolve it. For example, if a parent calls and leaves the message that she is upset with the homework policy in her child's math class, you need to know the specific problem regarding the homework policy. Is the problem with the amount of homework, the type of homework, or the complexity of the homework? Communicating with the parent in person, over the phone, or through e-mail will be the only way to accurately identify the problem.

Getting the Parent's Viewpoint

In the event of a problem or disagreement, find out exactly what the problem is from the parent's viewpoint. Regardless of the type of communication mode implemented, any contact made soon after finding out there is a problem is essential. First of all, it shows the parent that you are interested in her viewpoint and want to understand her concerns. It will also allow you to address a situation early so that the perceived problem does not become a bigger issue. Given the information you have about the parent, you should contact her with the mode of communication she prefers, and then strive to develop possible solutions to the problem.

Identifying Possible Solutions

At this stage, it is your responsibility to come up with possible solutions to the conflict. A suggested technique to try is brainstorming—simply make a list of every possible solution that could be implemented. Parents and professionals also need to provide input on possible solutions to the problem. The more comprehensive your list, the more solutions there will be to choose from. Remember, if both parties agree on a resolution and it is not successful, you can meet again to discuss progress or lack of progress and choose another way to solve the problem.

• •

Brainstorming: Process or procedure used to generate ideas or come up with solutions to specific problems. Brainstorming can be done individually or in a group setting.

• •

Reaching a Consensus

To reach a consensus regarding a conflict or problem, it is important to gather all available information. In almost all cases a solution can be derived, but you need to include all of the impacted people from the very beginning. Ultimately, every decision you make impacts the student. When coming to a consensus, the student has to be the first consideration. How will the solution impact his learning? Will the solution benefit or possibly have a negative impact on the student? How will the student move toward being successful? When making a decision about the student, his individual needs should be considered. Depending on the age and maturity level of the student, it may be beneficial to consult with the child about his specific needs in relationship to the issue being addressed. We want all students to experience success, so considering their needs is crucial in this process. See Table 3 for an example of handling a conflict or problem with parents.

• •

Consensus: Agreement or opinion that is reached by a group.

• •

Respecting Confidentiality

Student information is confidential. Be careful about the information that you disclose about a student. Each student has a personal file, but there is limited access to it depending on who is working with the student. For additional information about confidentiality, read Chapter 4, which discusses the laws that specifically relate to privacy and confidentiality. Specific categories of information you should be aware of include (a) sharing of personal information, (b) discussing the student's disability, and (c) supporting information that is located on the IEP.

• •

Confidential information: Information that should not be made available to the public.

• •

Table 3
Example of Handling a Conflict/Problem With Parents

Stage	Example
Identifying the problem	Parent calls the teacher and leaves a message saying that she has an issue with what is going on in math. Specifically, it appears there is a problem with her child's homework.
Getting the parent's viewpoint	Contact the parent to find out the specific complaint about the homework. The teacher calls the parent and finds out that the student is taking 2–3 hours per evening to complete his math homework. The parent has talked to other parents, and their children take about 30 minutes on the homework.
Identifying possible solutions	As a teacher, consider watching the student complete his homework in class to look for possible solutions. There are a couple of possible solutions in this example. Could the student use a calculator? Could the assignment be shortened? Does the student have a math disability? Analyze the amount and type of math problems and see if there is another alternative to the length or complexity of the assignment.
Reaching a consensus	The student needs to do the homework for two reasons. The first is to practice the new math skills. The second is so the teacher can see if the student understands the material taught in class. What can be done to make the homework more manageable? After speaking with the student, parent, and math teacher, it was decided that the length of the assignment would be shortened. Instead of 6–8 problems in each area the student would only have to do 3–4 problems. In addition, the day after the assignment was given there would be a review session with the special education teacher prior to math class.

Sharing of Personal Information

Maintaining confidentiality of student and family information is a very important skill inclusive classroom teachers must possess. Obviously, this information can be shared with members of the IEP team, as well as those teachers and related school personnel that directly work with a child, but others should not be made privy to this information. This information includes (a) name, (b) birth date, (c) address, (d) age, (e) ethnicity, and (f) native language. Although much of this information could be accessed from general school records, other schoolteachers and educational personnel should not have access to this information if they are not directly working with the student.

People-First Language

Information about a student's disability must also remain confidential. Those who are not directly providing services to the student should not have access to this information. Teachers should also consider whether it is actually important to specify the specific disability (i.e., learning disability, emotional/behavior disorder, cognitive disability, autism) to other teachers. Unfortunately, when a student is identified with a specific disability, some teachers may have preconceived expectations about her ability and performance. This could result in lower expectations being placed on a child or even the development of a negative perception of a child's personality before actually meeting the child and having the opportunity to work with her.

When discussing a disability, individuals should use people-first language. This means that a child is addressed as an individual first, and then the specific disability follows (e.g., "a student with learning disabilities" as opposed to "a learning disabled student"). This will ensure that the student is always seen first prior to the disability. Using people-first language provides a more accurate way of communicating about the student and a more respectful one as well. Examples of people-first language can be seen in Table 4.

• •

People-first language: In oral and written speech, addressing a child as an individual first and then following with the specific disability.

• •

Recognizing the Impact of a Disability

Another aspect to recognize with regard to students with disabilities is the impact the disability may have on the student's parents and siblings. This may change how you communicate with parents. It is also important to understand

Table 4
Examples of People-First Language

People-First Language to Use	Instead of Labels That Stereotype and Devalue Such as
• people/individuals with disabilities • an adult who has a disability • a child with a disability	• the handicapped • the disabled
• people/individuals without disabilities • typical kids	• normal people/healthy individuals • atypical kids
• people with intellectual and developmental disabilities • he or she has a cognitive impairment • a person who has Down syndrome	• the mentally retarded; retarded people • he or she is retarded; the retarded • he or she's a Downs kid; a Mongoloid; a Mongol
• a person who has autism	• autistic
• people with a mental illness • a person who has an emotional disability • a person with a psychiatric illness/disability	• the mentally ill; the emotionally disturbed • is insane; crazy; demented; a psycho • a maniac; a lunatic
• a person who has a learning disability	• the learning disabled
• a person who is deaf • he or she has a hearing impairment/loss • a man/woman who is hard of hearing	• the deaf
• person who is deaf and cannot speak • a person who has a speech disorder • a person who uses a communication device • a person who uses synthetic speech	• is deaf and dumb • mute
• a person who is blind • a person who has a visual impairment • a child who has low vision	• the blind
• a person who has epilepsy • people with a seizure disorder	• an epileptic • a victim of epilepsy
• a person who uses a wheelchair • people who have a mobility impairment • a person who walks with crutches	• a person who is wheelchair bound • a person who is confined to a wheelchair • a cripple
• a person who has quadriplegia • people with paraplegia	• a quadriplegic • the paraplegic
• he or she is of small or short stature	• a dwarf or midget
• he or she has a congenital disability	• he or she has a birth defect
• accessible buses, bathrooms, etc. • reserved parking for people with disabilities	• handicapped buses, bathrooms, etc. • handicapped parking

Adapted from "People First Language" by Texas Council for Developmental Disabilities, n.d., http://www.txddc.state.tx.us/resources/publications/pfanguage.asp. Copyright 2011 by Texas Council for Developmental Disabilities. Adapted with permission.

the situation the parents and siblings of the student face at home. An understanding and compassion for what happens at home can go a long way in becoming a more effective teacher.

Parental Time Commitment

To fully understand the changes a student with a disability may have on his family, it is important for teachers to know the characteristics that are associated with a specific disability. There are different levels of severity for each disability, so the impact will vary for each family. For example, a learning disability may be mild or severe. It may be the difference between a child being fully independent (he can basically do everything himself) to fully dependent (he needs help with everything) on the family. The more dependent the child with a disability is on the family, the more time the family will spend meeting the child's needs. See Table 5 for common characteristics of children with specific disabilities.

Depending on the disability, the parents could have to spend extraordinary amounts of time just meeting the needs of the child. This takes time away from other family members. It may also mean that parents might not be able to respond to you as quickly as you would prefer. Understanding the family structure and time commitment of the parents is important to be aware of when working with families. This must be remembered when trying to facilitate constant and frequent communication. Sometimes parents will need outside support for the care of their child. It would be worthwhile to research service providers in the community who specialize in childcare for children with disabilities. This information comes in handy when parents indicate that they need a break away from their hectic schedules. Another thought would be to recommend afterschool programs that are available to help the child with her homework. If you are near a university, research the possibility of getting tutors or childcare providers from professional student organizations within the university. As a teacher, working with parents as well as students is instrumental in the success of all members of the family.

Impact on Siblings

A child with a disability impacts everyone in the family. As a result, siblings may feel that their needs are seen as secondary due to the time commitments made to the sibling with a disability. Because the family spends so much time meeting the needs of the child with a disability, time and attention given to siblings may be reduced. The sibling might be limited in his ability to participate in athletics, music, plays, or other afterschool activities because of the responsibility to help his sibling or because of his parents' inability to transport him to events due to time commitments already made to ensure his sibling has the

Table 5
Common Characteristics of Children With Specific Disabilities

Special Need	Characteristics
Children With Autism Spectrum Disorder	• Develop language differently than most children (most often delayed) • Experience minimum social development (not spontaneous) • Often participate in repetitive behaviors (such as echolalia, the repetition of sounds) • Often exhibit disruptive behavior (especially in classrooms) • Are highly sensitive to sensory experiences and movement • Demonstrate irregular intellectual development (unusual patterns of strengths and weaknesses)
Children With Attention Deficit/ Hyperactivity Disorder (ADHD)	• Show inattentive behavior • Exhibit hyperactive and impulsive behaviors • Experience difficulty in relationships with adults and peers • Often have low self-esteem
Children With Speech and/ or Language Impairments	• Possess disorders that affect the rate and rhythm of speech • Often cannot produce various sounds • Often omit or add sounds when producing words • Often distort sounds • May have voice disorders, such as an unusually high pitch or nasality (when sounds seem to be emitted through children's noses) • May possess limited ability to express themselves (language impairment) • May experience difficulty following directions or understanding verbal emotions (language impairment)
Children With Hearing Impairments	• Often ignore adults and/or peers when they are spoken to • May exhibit confusion when responding to questions or instructions • Often cannot hear unless they are facing the speaker • Often demonstrate unclear language production • Often struggle with social behaviors • May be unable to hear in a noisy classroom (sensory defensiveness)
Children With Vision Impairments	• Have impairments ranging from minor deficits to total blindness • May experience different levels of eye function from day to day • Are visually affected by classroom lighting, time of day, and weather • May be hypersensitive to touch (tactile defensiveness) • May have other disabilities (up to 60% of children with visual impairments do) • Tend to rely on nonverbal senses to receive information
Children With Orthopedic Impairments (Physical Impairments)	• May have a congenital condition • May have cerebral palsy, spina bifida, muscular dystrophy, and/or fractures or burns; orthopedic impairments vary widely depending on the specific type of orthopedic impairment (congenital conditions or as a result of accidents) • May experience paralysis, tightness or weakness in the legs or throughout the body, or chronic inflammation and pain of the joints • May or may not have a learning disability

Table 5. Common Characteristics of Children With Specific Disabilities, continued	
Special Need	**Characteristics**
Children With Developmental Delays	• Acquire skills and knowledge at a delayed rate • May have problems with hearing and vision • Have difficulty attending to classroom activities • Might be a result of environmental factors • Have delayed language development
Children With Traumatic Brain Injury	• May have experienced an external physical injury • Have difficulty gaining educational achievement • May exhibit motor dysfunction • Often have problems with attention and memory • May have difficulties in communicating with others • May exhibit social and emotional changes

From *Successful Inclusion Strategies for Early Childhood Teachers* by C. G. Simpson and L. Warner, 2010, p. xiii, Waco, TX: Prufrock Press. Copyright 2010 Prufrock Press. Reprinted with permission.

services she needs. Teachers in inclusive classrooms need to be aware of this and be able to offer suggestions to parents to make opportunities more readily available to siblings. In addition, teachers may be aware of other community programs that could provide support for siblings of students with disabilities. Again, we want to clarify that having a child with a disability impacts many different aspects of the family, including how and when the parents communicate with the school.

SURVIVAL SECRETS OF TEACHERS

Emma, Middle School Special Education Teacher

What Is Your Current Position and How Long Have You Been Teaching?

Currently, I teach sixth-, seventh-, and eighth-grade special education in inclusive and resource room settings. I have been teaching for 2 years.

What Were Some of the Issues You Faced With Parent Relationships as a First-Year Teacher?

There were not a lot of issues that I faced, but one of the main issues was that many times parents were intimidated by the whole special education process. Working on IEPs, data, goals, strategies, and so on can be very overwhelming. To resolve this issue, I created a glossary that listed and defined all of the terminology so someone without a background in special education could understand it. Another issue was that many parents felt that they had no input in or that they were not a part of the decision-making process. I addressed this issue through constant communication and trying to keep them abreast as to the current status and progress being made by their child. The last issue I faced was that the previous relationships some parents had with special education teachers were not positive. It took me a long time to break through these barriers, but I tried to be open, accessible, and honest with them, and in some cases I am still trying to make progress in this area with parents.

How Did You Make Yourself Accessible to Parents?

At the beginning of the school year, I contacted all of the parents of the students on my caseload. I introduced myself as the special education teacher who would be working with their child and told them that my goal was to help their child learn to the best of his ability. I explained my role to them—I would be co-teaching with a general education teacher for a portion of my time, and other times I would be working with their children in a resource room setting providing help, guidance, and strategies to be successful. I also shared my contact information and told them they could contact me for any reason. Last of all, I gave them an opportunity to tell me about their child. I asked them to give me their perception of their child's abilities, strengths, and areas he had difficulties with. I found this approach worked very well, and as a result, I had a good rapport and open communication with most of the parents of my students.

What Advice Would You Give Future Teachers About Connecting With Parents?

That is simple—multiple methods. Each set of parents seems to be unique in how often they want communication and in what way they want their communication to take place. At the beginning of the school year, connect with parents of students on your caseload and find out their preferences. Don't be afraid of the parents, and be proactive taking the first step. Find answers to the following questions: "How important is communication to them?" "How often would they like to be contacted?" "What type of communication do they prefer?" Once you get this information, make sure you follow through and communicate with the parents in the method that they prefer. Providing parents with consistent communication will prove to be a great benefit to you and your student and will probably make it easier to deal with problems when they occur. When there is a problem that needs to be addressed, establishing a good, positive avenue for communication encourages parents to be more open when discussing ways to resolve issues.

Conclusion

It is very important for inclusion teachers to establish positive relationships with parents. To be successful in the classroom, one major component is the ability to communicate effectively and consistently with parents. Find out the best way to communicate with each of your parents and then add other ways to make sure you are communicating through multiple means. For example, you could contact parents by phone and through e-mail. Just like you would gain trust with a student, you must do this with parents as well. No matter if you are dealing with a problem or conflict, confidentiality, or how other siblings are impacted, you need to remain open and accessible. It is important to gain the trust of your students and their parents, as parents can definitely have a positive impact on the academic success of their children. Effective and constant communication is essential for inclusion classroom teachers.

Survival Tips

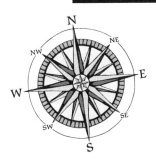

- Remember—parents are the experts on their children.
- Open lines of communication between teachers and parents are key in addressing the needs of the student.
- Share free resources that may be available within the community for parents who need additional support beyond what the school can offer.

Survival Toolkit

Professional Organizations to Support You in Working With Parents and Families

- National PTA: http://www.pta.org

- National Education Association: http://www.nea.org
- National Association for the Education of Young Children: http://www.naeyc.org
- Council for Exceptional Children: http://www.cec.sped.org
- National Coalition for Parental Involvement in Education: http://www.ncpie.org

Websites to Support You in Working With Parents and Families

- Teacher-Parent Collaboration: http://www.teachervision.fen.com/education-and-parents/resource/3730.html
- Family, School and Community Collaboration Dialogue Guides: http://www.ideapartnership.org/index.php?option=com_content&view=category&id=261&Itemid=111
- Parent/Professional Collaboration: http://www.ncset.org/topics/family/default.asp?topic=29
- Communicating With Families: http://www2.scholastic.com/browse/collection.jsp?id=337

Books to Help You in Working With Parents and Families

Friend, M., & Cook, L. (2009). *Interactions: Collaboration skills for school professionals* (6th ed.). Upper Saddle River, NJ: Prentice Hall.

Gorman, J. C. (2004). *Working with challenging parents of students with special needs*. Thousand Oaks, CA: Corwin Press.

Porter, L. (2008). *Teacher-parent collaboration: Early childhood to adolescence*. Victoria, Australia: ACER Press.

Smith, T. E. C., Gartin, B. C., Murdick, N. L., & Hilton, A. (2005). *Families and children with special needs: Professional and family partnerships*. Upper Saddle River, NJ: Prentice Hall.

4 Special Education and the Law

Special education law is one area in your teacher preparation program that may not have been addressed in much detail. Knowing the laws that drive the field of special education is very important for special education teachers. Whether it involves advocating for one of your students or communicating with other teachers or parents, understanding legal issues specifically related to students with special needs is critical. Administrators will expect all special educators to have a basic knowledge and understanding of the Individuals with Disabilities Education Improvement Act (IDEA, 2004), Section 504 of the Rehabilitation Act of 1973, and the Americans with Disabilities Act (ADA, 1990). In addition, you will need to be able to relate the specific elements of the law to the students in your classrooms.

Individuals with Disabilities Education Improvement Act

One of the most prevalent pieces of special education law is the Individuals with Disabilities Education Improvement Act (IDEA), signed into law on December 3, 2004, by President George W. Bush. The provisions of the act became effective on July 1, 2005, with the exception of some of the elements pertaining to the definition of a "highly qualified teacher" that took effect upon the signing of the act. The final regulations were published on August 14, 2006. This information is important to know, but it is more important for a teacher to understand the parts of the legislation that will impact instruction and placement of children in inclusive classrooms.

IDEA (2004) listed 13 separate categories of disabilities under which children may be eligible for special education and related services. See Table 6 for a listing of the 13 separate categories. To determine if a child is eligible for classification under one of the 13 areas of exceptionality, an individualized evaluation or assessment of the child will be conducted. Specific assessments will be chosen based on the problems the child is presenting. The results of these assessments will be used to determine whether or not the child has a specific disability. It is also important to note that a diagnosis is different from the actual educational disabilities as indicated above. Table 7 shows examples of diagnoses and how they translate into legal definitions of educational disabilities.

We suggest that you learn more information about the different diagnostic instruments that are used for children with specific disabilities in your classroom and how the assessment results will help you develop effective interventions in your classroom setting. Whenever legal issues are discussed, it is necessary to address the processes required when a student's assessment, placement, or IEP development are in question.

Evaluation and Classification

In this book, we have dedicated Chapter 6 to the assessment of students served in the inclusive classroom and how assessment impacts the child related to the curriculum of the school and immediate classroom learning. That chapter also looks at how the teacher can monitor student achievement and progress. This particular section will address assessment in terms of evaluation and classification and its relationship to legal issues. For the purpose of this section, evaluation in special education is defined as the process used to determine a child's specific learning strengths and needs and to determine whether or not a child is eligible for special education services. This process involves collecting information about a student for the purpose of making classification and placement decisions.

The importance of the initial evaluation should never be underestimated. In an inclusive education setting, you will work with many professionals as a part of a team, often referred to as a multidisciplinary team, which will determine what disability, if any, is present in a student. Although this initial evaluation may be done prior to the student being served in your classroom, it is important to have a basic understanding of those skills that the decision makers possess. The skills they must possess are very important in order to offer a child the most global, accurate, and practical evaluation possible. The development of these

Table 6
Special Education Categories

Category	Definition
Autism	A developmental disability significantly affecting verbal and nonverbal communication and social interaction, generally evident before age 3
Deafness	A hearing impairment that is so severe that the child is impaired in processing linguistic information, with or without amplification
Deaf-blindness	Simultaneous hearing and visual impairments
Hearing impairment	An impairment in hearing, whether permanent or fluctuating
Intellectual disabilities (mental retardation)	Significantly subaverage general intellectual functioning existing concurrently with deficits in adaptive behavior
Multiple disabilities	The manifestation of two or more disabilities (such as intellectual disabilities-blindness), the combination of which requires special accommodation for maximal learning
Orthopedic impairment	Physical disabilities, including congenital impairments, impairments caused by disease, and impairments from other causes
Other health impairment	Having limited strength, vitality, or alertness due to chronic or acute health problems; includes Attention Deficit/Hyperactivity Disorder
Serious emotional disturbance	A disability where a child of typical intelligence has difficulty, over time and to a marked degree, building satisfactory interpersonal relationships; responds inappropriately behaviorally or emotionally under normal circumstances; demonstrates a pervasive mood of unhappiness; or has a tendency to develop physical symptoms or fears
Specific learning disability	A disorder in one or more of the basic psychological processes involved in understanding or in using language, spoken or written, which may manifest itself in an imperfect ability to listen, think, speak, read, write, spell, or do mathematical calculations
Speech or language impairment	A communication disorder such as stuttering, impaired articulation, a language impairment, or a voice impairment
Traumatic brain injury	An acquired injury to the brain caused by an external physical force, resulting in total or partial functional disability, psychosocial impairment, or both
Visual impairment	A visual difficulty (including blindness) that, even with correction, adversely affects a child's educational performance

From Maryville City Schools (2005).

Table 7
How Diagnoses Translate to Legal Definitions of Disabilities

Examples of Diagnoses That Translate to:	Legal Definition of Disability
dyslexia, dysgraphia, dyscalculia, learning disorder, reading disorder, disorder of written expression, math disorder; learning disorder, not otherwise specified (NOS); nonverbal learning disorder or disability	The term Specific Learning Disability means a disorder in one or more of the basic psychological processes involved in understanding or in using language, spoken or written, which may manifest itself in the imperfect ability to listen, think, speak, read, write, spell, or do mathematical calculations. The term includes such conditions as perceptual disabilities, brain injury, minimal brain dysfunction, dyslexia, and developmental aphasia. The term does not include a learning problem that is primarily the result of visual, hearing, or motor disabilities, of mental retardation, of emotional disturbance, or of environmental, cultural, or economic disadvantage (108th Congress, 2004).
autism; pervasive developmental disorder, NOS; childhood disintegrative disorder; Rett syndrome; Asperger's syndrome	Autism means a developmental disability significantly affecting verbal and nonverbal communication and social interaction, generally evident before age 3 that adversely affects a child's educational performance. Other characteristics often associated with autism are engagement in repetitive activities and stereotyped movements, resistance to environmental change or change in daily routines, and unusual responses to sensory experiences. Autism does not apply if a child's educational performance is adversely affected primarily because the child has an emotional disturbance. A child who manifests the characteristics of autism after age 3 could be identified as having autism (U.S. Department of Education, 2006).
anxiety; depression; oppositional defiant disorder; mood disorder; conduct disorder; personality disorder	Emotional disturbance means a condition exhibiting one or more of the following characteristics over a long period of time and to a marked degree that adversely affects a child's educational performance: (a) an inability to learn that cannot be explained by intellectual, sensory, or health factors; (b) an inability to build or maintain satisfactory interpersonal relationships with peers and teachers; (c) inappropriate types of behavior or feelings under normal circumstances; (d) a general pervasive mood of unhappiness or depression; and (e) a tendency to develop physical symptoms or fears associated with personal or school problems. Emotional disturbance also includes schizophrenia. The term does not apply to children who are socially maladjusted, unless it is determined that they have an emotional disturbance (U.S. Department of Education, 2006).
cerebral palsy; spina bifida; use of walker, wheelchair, or other mobility device; poliomyelitis; bone tuberculosis; amputations, and fractures or burns that cause contractures	Orthopedic impairment defined as a severe orthopedic impairment that adversely impacts a child's educational performance. The term includes impairments caused by a congenital anomaly, impairments caused by disease, and impairments from other causes (U.S. Department of Education, 2006).
anxiety; Attention Deficit/Hyperactivity Disorder (ADD, ADHD); asthma; seizure disorder/epilepsy; lead poisoning; diabetes; Tourette's syndrome; sickle cell anemia; a heart condition; hemophilia; leukemia; nephritis; rheumatic fever	Other Health Impairment means having limited strength, vitality, or alertness, including a heightened alertness to environmental stimuli, that results in limited alertness with respect to the educational environment, that is due to chronic or acute health problems and adversely affects a child's educational performance (U.S. Department of Education, 2006).

Table 7. How Diagnoses Translate to Disabilities, continued.

Examples of Diagnoses That Translate to:	Legal Definition of Disability
Genetic disorders; Fragile X; Down's syndrome; phenylketonuria (PKU)	Mental retardation defined as "... significantly subaverage general intellectual functioning, existing concurrently with deficits in adaptive behavior and manifested during the developmental period, that adversely affects a child's educational performance" (National Dissemination Center for Children With Disabilities, 2004, p. 1).
Any eye-related problem that causes vision problems, does not include eye tracking for reading. May include congenital or injury-related conditions.	Blind or visually impaired defined as an impairment in vision that, even with correction, adversely affects a child's educational performance. The term includes both partial sight and blindness (U.S. Department of Education, 2006).
Any hearing loss, caused by injury or birth, with or without correction; children who wear Cochlear Implants for a variety of reasons	Deafness means a hearing impairment that is so severe that the student is impaired in processing linguistic information through hearing, with or without amplification; and adversely affects the student's educational performance (Maryland State Department of Education, 2000).
Dyspraxia, apraxia; central auditory processing disorder; articulation disorder, communication disorders, oral-motor disorders	Speech or language impairment means a communication disorder, such as stuttering, impaired articulation, a language impairment, or a voice impairment, that adversely affects a child's educational performance (U.S. Department of Education, 2006).
More than one diagnosis	Multiple disabilities means concomitant impairments (e.g., mental retardation-blindness or mental retardation-orthopedic impairment), the combination of which causes such severe educational needs that they cannot be accommodated in special education programs solely for one of the impairments. Multiple disabilities does not include deaf-blindness (108th Congress, 2004).
Any delay in any area, only applies federally to children to 9 years old. This does not apply in every state.	Developmental delay defined as children ages 3–9 experiencing developmental delays; a child who is experiencing developmental delays, as defined by the state and as measured by appropriate diagnostic instruments and procedures, in one or more of the following areas: physical development, cognitive development, communication development, social or emotional development, or adaptive development; and who, by reason thereof, needs special education and related services (IDEA, 2004).
A blow or trauma to the head that can be identified, including in utero	Traumatic brain injury means an acquired injury to the brain caused by an external physical force, resulting in total or partial functional disability or psychosocial impairment, or both, that adversely affects a child's educational performance. Traumatic brain injury applies to open or closed head injuries resulting in impairments in one or more areas, such as (but not limited to) cognition; language; memory; reasoning; sensory, perceptual, and motor abilities; physical functions; information processing; and speech. Traumatic brain injury does not apply to brain injuries that are congenital or degenerative or to brain injuries induced by birth trauma (108th Congress, 2004).

Table 8
Description of Assessment Skills

Assessment skill	Definition
Collection	Gathering information about a child from many sources such as school records, observation, parent intakes, and teacher reports
Analysis	Processing and understanding patterns in a child's educational, social, developmental, environmental, medical, and emotional history
Evaluation	Evaluating a child's academic, intellectual, psychological, emotional, perceptual, language, cognitive, and medical development in order to determine areas of strengths and weaknesses
Determination	Determining the presence of a suspected disability and understanding the criteria that constitute each category
Recommendation	Making recommendations concerning educational placement and programs to the school, teachers, and parents

Note. From National Association of Special Education Teachers (2006).

skills should include a good working knowledge of the following components of the assessment process in order to determine the presence of a suspected disability. See Table 8 for a description of assessment skills.

Assessment has many purposes, but in educational settings it serves five primary purposes, including:

- screening and identification (to screen children and identify those who may be experiencing delays or learning problems);
- eligibility and diagnosis (to determine whether an individual child has a disability and is eligible for special education services and to diagnose the specific nature of the student's problems or disability);
- IEP development and placement (to provide detailed information so that an IEP may be developed and appropriate decisions may be made about the child's educational placement);
- instructional planning (to develop and plan instruction appropriate to the child's special needs); and
- evaluation (to evaluate the student's progress).

The last two purposes will be areas that you continue to reassess once the child is receiving special education services.

Individualized Education Program

Once a child is determined to have a specific disability and placed in the inclusive setting, a teacher must follow the recommendations included in a very important document—the student's IEP. Developed by professionals for the student, the IEP includes:

- present level of educational performance,
- statement of measurable annual goals,
- explanation of progress measurement,
- description of special education services,
- statement of participation in the regular education program,
- statement describing testing adaptations and modifications,
- statement of length and duration of services, and
- an IEP statement of transition.

Each of these components will be described more specifically below. We will also link the specific element discussed to your role as the inclusion teacher.

Present level of educational performance. Every IEP must include a description of the child's skills in all areas of concern and explain how the disability affects his progress in the general education curriculum. Statements should address academics, life skills, physical functioning, social and behavioral skills, and any other areas of concern affecting the child's ability to learn. IEP teams typically use formal assessments to determine the child's functioning and establish a baseline of performance. The team may also use anecdotal information and progress data from the child's classroom teachers to describe the child's skills. As the inclusive classroom teacher, you may be directly collecting the data that will support the determination of the child's present level of performance. It is an ongoing process, and your continued contribution to the IEP team will ensure that the child's educational performance is accurately represented.

• •

Present levels of performance: A description of the child's skills in all areas of concern that also explains how the disability affects his progress in the general education curriculum.

• •

Statement of measurable annual goals. The IEP also contains statements of a child's goals that are updated on at least a yearly basis. Goal statements specify what the child is expected to learn in the coming year. Goals include academic skills and may also include functional skills as appropriate. For children who participate in functional skills programs and who take alternate assessments, the IEP must also contain measurable short-term objectives that will be used to measure the child's progress toward reaching his annual goals. The goals for each new year will be based on the child's progress toward the previous year's goals. Your role will be not only to instruct the child on his goals, but to document the progress he is making toward reaching the goals and to make recommendations based on this information to formulate new goals.

Explanation of progress measurement. The IEP must contain an explanation of how progress toward goals and objectives will be measured and describe how that information will be reported to parents. Each teacher has her own method of communication to notify parents of students' progress. As an inclusion teacher, you will be reporting the progress of all of the students in your classroom. However, particular attention must be given to those students with special needs to ensure that the information is reported as described in the IEP.

Description of special education services. The IEP must also include a description of the student's special education program, specially designed instruction, and related services the child will receive to help him progress toward meeting his educational goals. The amount of time he will receive services and the setting in which they will be provided must also be described. This explanation may cause confusion with teachers, as they often relate special education programs to a self-contained special education setting. This is not the case—a special education program for a child may very likely be a program designed to be implemented in the inclusive classroom. In preparing this portion of the IEP, you, as the inclusion teacher, must be prepared to indicate how your classroom instruction is adapted or modified to help the individual child meet his educational goals.

Statement of participation in the regular education program. To ensure that children are educated in the least restrictive environment (LRE) to the greatest extent appropriate, the IEP team must consider if and how the child will participate in the general education program with children without disabilities. The IEP must specify the amount of time a child will participate in regular education programs and explain the rationale for that decision. In a fully inclusive classroom, the documentation here may simply state that the child is educated in the LRE (in this case, the general education inclusive setting) for the full hours allocated in the school day. More detail regarding the LRE will be provided later in this chapter.

• •

Least restrictive environment (LRE): The environment that allows children with disabilities to be educated to the maximum extent possible with typically developing children.

• •

Statement describing testing adaptations and modifications. The IEP must explain what types of testing adaptations and modifications will be used with the student and why they are necessary. If the child will participate in alternative assessment, the rationale for that decision must be included in the IEP. If a child is receiving any specialized adaptation on statewide assessments, those same adaptations should mirror the ones used in the classroom on an ongoing basis. If a student does not need these adaptations in the classroom setting for similar assessments, it would be hard to justify that the child needs the particular adaptation for a statewide or districtwide assessment.

• •

Modification: An actual change to the curriculum. This might mean that the student will work in a lower level book instead of the one at grade level or the student will be given different questions on assessments and homework.

• •

Statement of length and duration of services. The IEP must include projected beginning and ending dates of service, the frequency of the services, where they will be delivered, and how long they will be provided. It is difficult to make this determination in the initial process, but as you spend more time with a student, you will be able to make recommendations based on the progress the student is making in your classroom setting.

Statement of transition. For teachers who teach at the middle school and high school level, you must consider your role in the statement of transition. Beginning no later than age 16, the IEP must include measurable goals for the student's anticipated postsecondary program and a description of the services needed for the child to reach those goals. In the transition plan, transition goals and services focus on instruction and support services needed to help the student move from the school environment into a job and to help her advocate for herself in college, a vocational program, or another program designed to promote independent living.

• •

Postsecondary education: Educational institutions beyond high school that have an academic, vocational, or professional focus.

Transition plan: Components of the IEP that relate to postschool life, including multiyear course of study, identification of postschool outcomes, identification of transition-related assessments and results of those assessments, multiyear transition activities, and services that will facilitate the desired postschool outcomes and related annual goals and objectives.

Postschool outcomes: Outcomes achieved by young adults with disabilities after exiting secondary school, including employment, independent living, and postsecondary education and training.

• •

Least Restrictive Environment

As part of IDEA, the LRE is identified as one of the six principles that govern the education of students with disabilities and other special needs. By law, schools are required to provide a free appropriate public education (FAPE) in the least restrictive environment that is appropriate to the individual student's needs.

Least restrictive environment means that a student who has a disability should have the opportunity to be educated with her peers without disabilities to the greatest extent appropriate. A student with a disability should have access to the general education curriculum, extracurricular activities, or any other program that her typical peers would be able to access. The student should be provided with supplementary aids and services necessary to achieve her educational goals if placed in a setting with peers without disabilities. Should the nature or severity of the disability prevent the student from achieving these goals in a regular education setting, then the student would be placed in a more restrictive environment such as a resource room or self-contained classroom. Generally, the less opportunity a student has to interact and learn with peers who do not have disabilities, the more restrictive the placement. In meeting the needs of students with disabilities in the LRE, many teachers are now serving in the role of a co-teacher in the general education inclusive classroom.

A child's IEP team is responsible for determining the most appropriate educational placement in the least restrictive environment that can meet the student's educational needs. With the differences in needs and interests among students with disabilities, a single definition of what an LRE will be for all students does not exist. Many factors need to be considered when determining the LRE for students with special needs. Some of these factors include:

- the student's ability to focus,
- the type of skills needed to learn,
- how much individually designed instruction is needed, and
- other educational issues unique to each child.

In addition, a child's IEP team determines LRE based on:

- IEP requirements,
- the amount of direct instruction the child needs,
- the setting most likely to help the child achieve his goals,
- the school facilities needed to support the child's learning, and
- consideration of services in the child's home school.

School districts are required to provide a continuum of alternative placements available to meet the needs of all students. The full range of potential placements includes (a) full-time instruction in a general education classroom, (b) general education classroom with pull-out programs, (c) instruction in a

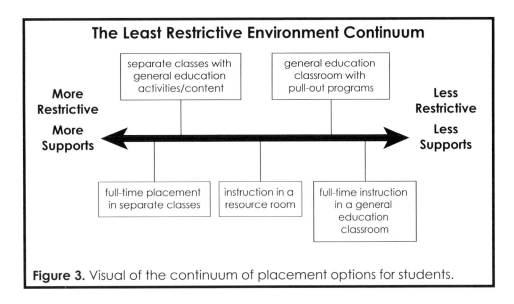

Figure 3. Visual of the continuum of placement options for students.

resource room, (d) separate classes with general education activities/content, and (e) full-time placement in separate classes. See Figure 3 for a visual depiction of this continuum.

The range of appropriate placements can also include combinations of those listed above. Choosing the appropriate LRE is important to ensure that each student receives the instruction he needs. Just to clarify, the LRE is not a specific placement. Rather, it is the most appropriate placement for a child depending on his needs. The placement (a) is a place in school where the IEP can be implemented, (b) is a flexible arrangement to meet the child's individual needs, and (c) can range from a separate classroom or school all day or part of the day to all-day placement in a regular classroom with appropriate supportive services.

Federal special education regulations require that a child with a disability will not be removed from the regular classroom to receive instruction unless his educational needs cannot be met with supplemental aides and services in regular classes. All placement decisions are made by the IEP team with parent input, are based on the IEP, and are reviewed at least annually. The IEP team should also consider any potentially negative effects of a placement on the child and on the adequacy of services the child may receive. As an inclusion teacher, you will need to be aware of how the LRE impacts the placement of a child in your classroom. In addition, as a member of the IEP team you will need to be able to make recommendations based on the information (data) you collect in your classroom.

Due Process

There will be times that the school and the parents cannot come to an agreement on the child's IEP. In those cases, IDEA includes procedures for resolving disputes between parents and schools. This can be done in a due processing hearing, which is a formal process that is intended to help facilitate appropriate decision making and services for children with disabilities. See Appendix A for a detailed description of due process.

• •

Due process hearing: Formal process that is intended to help facilitate appropriate decision making and services for children with disabilities.

• •

Confidentiality and Privacy

As an inclusive classroom teacher, you will be dealing with student's personal information daily. A child's educational records often contain private personal information about the child and the family. In the course of determining a child's eligibility for special education services and designing a program to meet the child's needs, schools may acquire information about the child's social and medical history. Sometimes, that record may include medical and other personal information about other members of the family. That information is private and confidential, and IDEA regulations outline a school district's obligations to protect the confidentiality of that information. Schools must protect the confidentiality of personally identifiable information when that information is collected, stored, disclosed, and destroyed. Personally identifiable means information that contains (a) the name of the child, the parent, or other family member; (b) the child's address; (c) a personal identifier such as a social security or student ID number; and (d) a list of personal characteristics or other information that would make it possible to identify the child with reasonable certainty.

Moreover, school districts must assign a specific person to be responsible for ensuring the confidentiality of personally identifiable information. Additionally, school staff members who collect or use this information must be trained in their state's confidentiality procedures under IDEA and the Family Education Rights and Privacy Act (FERPA) regulations. And finally, school districts must keep a current listing of the names and positions of all employees who have access to personally identifying information. That list must be available for public inspection.

• •

Family Education Rights and Privacy Act (FERPA): A U.S. federal law that protects the confidentiality of student education records.

• •

Of course, parents have the right to inspect and review their child's educational records. Parental access rights include the right to have information in the record interpreted or explained, the right to get copies of the record, and the right to have a representative of the parent review the records. Generally, personally identifiable information may not be disclosed without parental consent. For example, if a parent wanted the school district to allow the parent's representative or attorney to review the records, the parent would need to consent and authorize the district to provide that access. But information may be released without parent consent to officials of participating agencies in order to comply with IDEA.

Discipline

Another topic that teachers need to be aware of is discipline. When can a student be removed from class? When can a student be removed from the school? Is the disability of the student causing the negative behavior? The answers to these questions and more will follow.

Serious bodily injury. What happens if a child is suspected of causing serious bodily injury? School personnel may remove a student to an interim alternative educational setting for not more than 45 school days without regard to whether the behavior is determined to be a manifestation of the child's disability if the child:

- carries a weapon to or possesses a weapon at school, on school premises, or to or at a school function under the jurisdiction of a state educational agency (SEA) or a local educational agency (LEA);
- knowingly possesses or uses illegal drugs, or sells or solicits the sale of a controlled substance, while at school, on school premises, or to or at a school function under the jurisdiction of an SEA or an LEA; or
- has inflicted serious bodily injury upon another person while at school, on school premises, or at a school function under the jurisdiction of an SEA or an LEA.

Code of conduct. School personnel may remove a child with a disability who violates a code of student conduct from her current placement to an appropriate interim alternative educational setting, another setting, or suspension, for no more than 10 consecutive school days (to the extent those alternatives are applied to children without disabilities), and for additional removals of no more than 10 consecutive school days in that same school year for separate incidents of misconduct (as long as those removals do not constitute a change of placement).

For disciplinary actions that would change the child's current placement for more than 10 consecutive school days, if the behavior that gave rise to the violation of the school code is determined not to be a manifestation of the child's disability, school personnel may apply the relevant disciplinary procedures to children with disabilities in the same manner and for the same duration as the procedures would be applied to children without disabilities.

Required services. A public agency is only required to provide services during periods of removal to a child with a disability who has been removed from his current placement for 10 school days or less in that school year, if it provides services to a child without disabilities who is similarly removed. After a child with a disability has been removed from his current placement for 10 school days in the same school year, the public agency must provide services to him during any subsequent days of removal. A child with a disability who is removed from the child's current placement (a disciplinary change in placement for more than 10 consecutive school days where the behavior is determined not to be a manifestation of the disability or a removal for special circumstances related to drugs, weapons, or serious bodily injury) must:

- continue to receive education services (FAPE requirements), so as to enable the child to continue to participate in the general education curriculum (although in another setting), and to progress toward meeting the goals set out in the child's IEP; and
- receive, as appropriate, a functional behavioral assessment (FBA) and behavioral intervention services and modifications that are designed to address the behavior violation so that it does not recur.

After a child with a disability has been removed from his or her current placement for 10 school days in the same school year, if the current removal is for not more than 10 consecutive school days and is not a change of placement, then school personnel, in consultation with at least one of the child's teachers should determine the extent to which services are needed so as to enable the child to continue to participate in the general education curriculum (although in another setting), and to progress toward meeting the goals set out in the child's IEP.

Manifestation determinations. Within 10 school days of any decision to change the placement of a child with a disability because of a violation of a code of student conduct, the LEA, the parent, and relevant members of the child's IEP team (as determined by the parent and the LEA) must review all relevant information in the student's file, including the child's IEP, any teacher observations, and any relevant information provided by the parents to determine if:

- the conduct in question was caused by, or had a direct and substantial relationship to, the child's disability; or
- the conduct in question was the direct result of the LEA's failure to implement the IEP.

The conduct must be determined to be a manifestation of the child's disability if the LEA, the parent, and relevant members of the child's IEP team determine that a condition was met. If the LEA, the parent, and relevant members of the child's IEP team determine the condition was met, then the LEA must take immediate steps to remedy those deficiencies.

If the LEA, the parent, and relevant members of the IEP team make the determination that the conduct was a manifestation of the child's disability, the IEP team must either conduct a functional behavioral assessment (unless the LEA had conducted an FBA before the behavior that resulted in the change of placement occurred), and implement a behavior intervention plan (BIP) for the child or, if a BIP already has been developed, review the BIP, and modify it, as necessary, to address the behavior and return the child to the placement from which the child was removed (unless the parent and the LEA agree to a change of placement as part of the modification of the BIP).

Section 504

As a teacher in an inclusive classroom, you may also serve children who are receiving services under Section 504 of the Rehabilitation Act of 1973. Section 504 is a Civil Rights law that prohibits discrimination against individuals with disabilities and ensures that the child with a disability has equal access to an education. Unlike the Individuals with Disabilities Education Act (IDEA), Section 504 does not require the school to provide an IEP; however, the child may receive accommodations and modifications to address his educational needs, but with fewer procedural safeguards than are available to children with disabilities and their parents under IDEA.

• •

Section 504: A Civil Rights law that prohibits discrimination against individuals with disabilities and ensures that the child with a disability has equal access to an education.

• •

Section 504 is designed to eliminate discrimination on the basis of disability in any program or activity receiving federal financial assistance and also guarantees certain rights to individuals with disabilities, including the right to full participation and access to FAPE regardless of the nature or severity of the disability. In addition, Section 504 requires the provision of appropriate educational services that are designed to meet the individual needs of qualified students to the same extent that the needs of students without a disability are met. Essentially, Section 504 was designed to level the playing field and to ensure full participation by individuals with disabilities.

To qualify under Section 504, a student must (a) be determined to have a physical or mental impairment that *substantially limits* one or more major life activities including learning and behavior, (b) have a record of having such an impairment, or (c) be regarded as having such impairment. Section 504 ensures that a qualified child with a disability has equal access to education. The child may receive appropriate accommodations and modifications tailored to her individual needs.

Americans with Disabilities Act (ADA)

Another very important piece of legislation that teachers should be familiar with is the Americans with Disabilities Act (ADA), which was passed on July 26, 1990 as Public Law 101-336. ADA is landmark federal legislation that opens up services and employment opportunities to all Americans with disabilities. The law was written to strike a balance between the reasonable accommodation of citizens' needs and the capacity of private and public entities to respond. It is not an affirmative action law but is intended to eliminate illegal discrimination and level the playing field for disabled individuals.

ADA is the most comprehensive federal Civil Rights statute protecting the rights of people with disabilities. It affects access to employment; state and local government programs and services; places of public accommodation such as businesses, transportation, and nonprofit service providers; and telecommunications. The scope of the ADA in addressing the barriers to participation by people with disabilities in the mainstream of society is very broad. The ADA's Civil Rights protections are parallel to those that have previously been established by the federal government for women and racial, ethnic, and religious minorities.

• •

Americans with Disabilities Act of 1990 (ADA): A Civil Rights law that provides equal access and opportunity for and prevents discrimination against students with disabilities.

• •

SURVIVAL SECRETS OF TEACHERS

Samantha, Elementary Special Education Teacher

What Is Your Current Position and How Long Have You Been Teaching?

Currently I am in an elementary position working in inclusive classrooms with third-, fourth-, and fifth-grade students. I have been teaching for 4 years.

What Were Some of the Issues You Faced With Regard to Legal Issues as a First-Year Teacher?

I think the biggest issue was the fear that I would make a mistake and really screw something up [or that] my error would put the school or a student in a terrible situation. We have all read about teachers making a poor decision and some big court case evolving out of it. I didn't want to be that teacher. This never did happen, but the thought was constantly in my mind. I learned that the biggest reason teachers make errors is that they hurry and do something carelessly. When it came to contacting parents, developing IEPs, or filling out paperwork, I learned very early that I needed to plan time to do all of these things. I am a person who needs to think things through before she acts. By doing so, I was able to perform my role at the highest level possible, follow all of the legal guidelines, and help my students learn to their fullest potential.

How Did You Deal With Any Deficits in the Area of Legal Issues?

This was a huge area for me. I felt very unprepared, regarding legal issues, coming into teaching out of college. We touched upon legal aspects in various courses, but we never really went totally in depth about them. To learn more about legal issues, I bought a book about them, searched the web, and also asked for any documents my district might have. Through all of these materials, I became more comfortable with all of the legal issues associated with special education. I also asked other special education teachers when I had questions or was unclear about something. I learned very quickly that other teachers were quite helpful and actually liked helping other teachers. It made them feel sort of like experts. Plus, given that I was a brand-new teacher, I was open to any type of help, guidance, or feedback I could get.

What Advice Would You Give Future Teachers Regarding Legal Issues?

Legal issues are established and real. Don't be afraid for what might happen. Educate yourself about the legal issues involved with special education. Attend conference sessions on legal issues, read about them, and investigate the web. As a teacher you have dedicated yourself to teach others, but you have also dedicated yourself to be a lifelong learner. Things change in the legal system so be current, stay abreast of any changes, and communicate with others. Always be open to feedback and ask questions if you are uncertain. You are not expected to memorize every law, policy, or procedure related to special education, but you should know where to get the answer if you don't know it.

◇◇◇

Conclusion

The laws in special education are always expanding, and it is very important that teachers are aware of what the current status is regarding the law. This holds especially true for teachers in an inclusive classroom setting. We often hear that teachers are frightened away from teaching in an inclusive setting because of fear of failing to comply with the law. This fear should not be what drives your decision to educate students with disabilities in your classroom setting. Understanding the law and knowing that the law was designed to protect the rights of the students in your classroom, not to create stress on the classroom teachers, should reduce your fears. Just as the laws protect the rights of students, they also provide protection for the districts and the teachers serving the students.

Knowing and having a basic understanding of IDEA (e.g., evaluation and classification, IEPs, LRE, assessment, due process, confidentiality, discipline), Section 504, and ADA will prepare you to serve students, parents, and schools. These special education laws are relevant to your position and will impact the decisions you make regarding the students you are serving. This chapter has provided you with the basic information within these laws, but there will be times that you may need to access other resources for additional clarification. The best place to start would be your special education director.

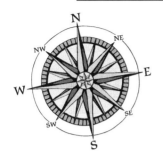

Survival Tips

- As a member of the IEP team, you need to be familiar with special education laws. This provides protection for you and your students.

- The IEP should not be written by one teacher. It is the responsibility of the IEP team to draft the document.

- The IEP is a legal document and must be implemented by all stakeholders listed in the IEP.

- Refer legal questions to the special education director/administrator. It is his responsibility to know the law in depth and to assist you in compliance issues.

Survival Toolkit

Professional Organizations to Support You in Understanding the Law

- American Federation of Teachers: http://www.aft.org

- National Education Association: http://www.nea.org

- Council for Exceptional Children: http://www.cec.sped.org

- United States Department of Education: http://www.ed.gov

- National Association of Special Education Teachers: http://www.naset.org

Websites to Help You Understand School Law

- Wrightslaw: http://www.wrightslaw.com

- National Dissemination Center for Children with Disabilities: http://www.nichcy.org

- U.S. Equal Employment Opportunity Commission: http://www.eeoc.gov

Books to Help You Understand School Law

Alexander, K., & Alexander, M. D. (2009). *The law of schools, students, and teachers in a nutshell* (4th ed.). St. Paul, MN: West.

Anderson, W., Chitwood, S., Hayden, D., & Takemoto, C. (2008). *Negotiating the special education maze: A guide for parents & teachers* (4th ed.). Bethesda, MD: Woodbine House.

Essex, N. L. (2010). *A teacher's pocket guide to school law* (2nd ed.). Upper Saddle River, NJ: Prentice Hall.

Weinfeld, R., & Davis, M. (2008). *Special needs advocacy resource book.* Waco, TX: Prufrock Press.

Wright, P. W. D., & Wright, P. D. (2007). *Wrightslaw: Special education law* (2nd ed.). Hartfield, VA: Harbor House Law Press.

5 Planning Academic Instruction

The previous chapter discussed IDEA and the components of the law that mandate that all children, including those without disabilities, are entitled to FAPE. One of the essential elements of this law is the requirement for students with disabilities to have an IEP. With each reauthorization of IDEA (1990, 1997, 2004), IEP requirements were adjusted to address the new challenges and needs of students with disabilities to further ensure the implementation of the law. In this chapter, we will expand on the implementation of the IEP including paperwork requirements, accommodations and modifications, lesson plan development, and components of effective instruction.

Beginning With the Individualized Education Program

The IEP is a written document required for each child who is found eligible to receive special education services and is used to plan academic instruction. The IEP provides information on the child's current levels of performance and directs the special services and supports that are provided to students who have IEPs. It includes provisions for defining annual goals, evaluating progress, and formalizing what FAPE constitutes for the student. Along with a description of the designated services, supports, and accommodations, the IEP defines how the child's progress toward meeting the IEP goals will be measured. Reports that show the progress the child is making on reaching her goals by the end of the year are given to parents. These progress reports should be sent as often as the parents of children without disabilities are informed of their children's progress.

• •

Accommodations: Changes in materials, instruction, or assessment that allow students to participate in and access general education without significantly altering the nature of the activity. It might mean that a student is given more time to complete assignments, a seat in the front of the class, or tests orally instead of on paper. It is not a change to what the student is required to learn.

• •

With the 2004 reauthorization of IDEA, the IEP continued to be the subject of revisions. These amendments included some revisions to the contents of the IEP as well as to the IEP meetings, as noted in Figure 4. The 2004 reauthorization of the law focused on ways to make the process of developing and revising the IEP more efficient. Some educators have treated the IEP as though it defines the curriculum for the child with disabilities, but the role of the IEP is to state services, supports, and framework for access to the general curriculum provided in the least restrictive environment for each child.

Writing the IEP

Most local education agencies use their own set of forms to develop the IEP to ensure it meets federal and state requirements. However, many school systems recently have moved to computer-based IEPs that are supposed to streamline the process and reduce the amount of teacher paperwork (see Appendix B for sample IEP forms). Most special education teachers would agree that one of the biggest challenges is managing the paperwork requirements of the IEP for all of the students on their caseloads. As a special education teacher, you must work with the team to develop the IEP, document progress toward IEP goals, ensure that all requirements of the IEP are being implemented within the required time frames, develop ongoing assessment and instructional procedures to be used with the student, and support the general education teachers who are required to implement the IEP within their classrooms. It is also your responsibility to make sure each teacher who is working with children who have IEPs has access to the plan, because they are also responsible for implementing it. For example, if a child has goals specific to math class, the math teacher needs to know what those goals are in order to address those deficits and show progress.

Content of IEPs:
- Present level of performance must include the child's academic achievement and functional performance.
- Annual goals must be measureable.
- Short-term objectives are required only for children who take alternative assessments.
- IEPs must describe how progress will be measured and when reports will be issued.

IEP Meetings:
- The teacher's attendance may be waived if:
  o the teacher's curriculum area is not addressed, or
  o a report based on the curriculum area is submitted prior to the meeting and is approved by the student's parents and the local education agency.

- Fifteen states may apply for an optional multiyear IEP pilot program. This means that, in some cases, annual IEP meetings may not be required and may be conducted no less than every 3 years.

Figure 4. IDEA (2004) amendments addressing changes in IEPs/meetings.

Clearly, as you can see, a great deal of paperwork is involved in this process. It takes a sound organizational system that incorporates a timeline to help you stay on track.

SURVIVAL SECRETS OF TEACHERS

Emily, Teacher in Self-Contained Classroom

What Has Been Your Experience in Writing IEPs?

When I began teaching 2 years ago, the district moved to a computerized program for completing IEPs. It was a big change from how they were previously done in the schools and how I learned to do them in college. At least all of the teachers were learning together, so that made it easier. In the process of writing my first IEP, I was very nervous. Fortunately, my mentor teacher was able to give me a lot of assistance in writing [the plans] and even sat in on my IEP meetings for the first year. The process has become easier as I have gotten used to the forms. Every student is different, and the IEP should be written with the specific student in mind. When developing a student's IEP, I write a draft of the student's level of performance and what the student needs to work on throughout the next year. During the meeting, the IEP team, which consists of the parent, general education teacher, special education teacher, LEA representative, related service individuals, and the student if appropriate, write the IEP together. The draft just gives us a starting point.

What Has Been Your Experience With IEP Meetings?

IEP meetings can be very insightful and encouraging especially if everyone's focus is in the student's best interest. It is one of the few times I get to talk with the parents about their child's specific goals and concerns. I also show them their child's work and the progress he is making. I lead the IEP meetings for the students on my caseload, although it is my goal that the IEP meetings be led by students. IEP meetings can get a little more difficult when you have forms to complete other than the standard IEP forms. For example, there are different procedures if the student transfers into the district from another county in the state or a different state, if the student is exiting the program, or if the student needs a behavior intervention plan. It can be challenging trying to complete these forms and discuss some of this information with the parent, but if you have a good support system within the school and at the central office, then they should be able to answer questions and give you the specific training you need.

What Type of Data Do You Collect During the School Year to Show You Are Implementing the IEP?

Collecting data is a struggle for me. Each student has specific goals and behaviors that need to be documented. I keep data sheets on positive and negative behavior and work samples of writing, math, science, and reading logs. Collecting data on reading, especially with students who are not currently reading, is very difficult so I made a chart that includes a scale of 1–9 to show their progress.

Student: _____

Date: _____

Reading Chart

	M	T	W	Th	F
1 = listening					
2 = looking at book					
3 = pointed to pictures					
4 = turned pages independently					
5 = pointed to words					
6 = repeated sounds after teacher					
7 = repeated words after teacher					
8 = read words aloud					
9 = read independently					

This allows me to show progress in my students' overall reading skills and their progress toward meeting their IEP reading goals. In addition to collecting data on academics, I keep a log of when parents are contacted and the outcome of the conversation. Data collection may seem time consuming but without it, we cannot show the progress our students have made and the amount of time and effort we have put into teaching each student.

Accommodations and Modifications

As part of the IEP, any accommodation or modification that is going to be part of the student's instructional plan has to be documented. Accommodations refer to the actual teaching supports and services that the student may require to successfully demonstrate learning. Accommodations should not change expectations for the grade-level curriculum. With many students with disabilities, accommodations are going to be implemented within the general education classroom. A significant number of these students will also take the statewide and districtwide assessments, so identifying strategies and adaptations that can be made to materials, tests, and instructional delivery will be key in the success of students with disabilities.

What Are Accommodations?

The student is accessing the general education curriculum, using:
- alternate acquisition modes such as calculators, computers, video/audiotape, books on tape, Braille readers, and adapted keyboards;
- content enhancements such as graphic organizers, study guides, and highlighters; and
- alternate response modes such as oral responses, computer responses, untimed responses, and work product options.

Figure 5. Accommodations in the classroom (Jitendra, Edwards, Choutka, & Treadway, 2002).

What Are Modifications?

Modifications are changes made to the general education curriculum, including:
- different materials such as:
  o alternative curriculum that is high interest but low demand, and
  o alternative instruction that is less content instruction but more explicit;

- different products such as different type of problems or alternative work products; and
- different content expectations including:
  o when decisions on what to teach are based on analyzing the content with respect to student's individualized objectives, and
  o course substitutions.

Figure 6. Modifications in the classroom (Jitendra et al., 2002).

Modifications refer to changes made to curriculum expectations in order to meet the needs of the student. Modifications are made when the expectations are beyond the student's level of ability. Modifications may be minimal or very complex and must be clearly identified in the IEP. Figures 5 and 6 provide examples for making accommodations or modifications in the classroom.

It is important to remember that adaptations made to instruction should be based on students' needs and instructional demands. The focus is to ensure that students with disabilities are successful in whatever classroom they are attending. As the special education teacher, you will be responsible for ensuring that each general education teacher who has a student with an IEP has a copy of the accommodations and modifications page from the IEP. Figure 7 shares an example of this page in the IEP. The information checked off on this page is

---

Curriculum/Classroom Accommodations and Modifications

Student Name: _____ *Date of IEP Meeting:*_____
Please check all that apply.

Flexible schedule
❑ Extended time
❑ Positive reinforcement

Alternate means of responding
❑ Opportunity to respond orally
❑ Use of scribe
❑ Student records answers on tape

Instruction
❑ Highlighted text/materials
❑ Reduced paper-and-pencil tasks
❑ Assignment notebook
❑ Taped lectures
❑ Shorter instructions
❑ Note taking
❑ Use of FM system

Testing
❑ Scribe
❑ Oral exams
❑ Exams read to student
❑ Extended time
❑ Individual or small group

Materials
❑ Spellcheckers
❑ Spelling dictionaries
❑ Accessible text (e.g., Braille, large print)
❑ Modified textbooks
❑ Calculators
❑ Assistive technology
❑ Keyboard modifications (e.g., touch screens, alternative input devices)

Other
❑ Behavior intervention plan (BIP)
❑ Class size
❑ Communication boards
❑ Bilingual dictionaries
❑ Preferential seating
❑ Other: _____

Figure 7. Template for accommodations and modifications.

---

specific to each student with an IEP and is decided by the IEP team. General education teachers are responsible for implementing the accommodations or modifications on this page. Additional modifications/accommodations for young children can be found in Table 9.

Writing Lesson Plans

As an inclusion teacher, it is easy to be overwhelmed with all of your new responsibilities, but because your ultimate goal is to be an effective classroom teacher, you need an instructional plan. The purpose of a written lesson plan is to assist teachers in identifying what they will teach and how they will teach it. Careful planning of instruction will also decrease or prevent some behavior problems. Early in your teaching career, you may begin by writing out

Table 9
Modifications and Accommodations for Young Children

Disability	Classroom Environment	Curriculum Content	Instruction/Evaluation
Autism Spectrum Disorder	• Organize seating arrangements and classroom furniture to meet the needs of all children (maintain the structure of the physical environment as well as instructional environment) • Seat the child near the teacher or peer buddy as necessary (to support the use of peer tutoring) • Include quiet areas in classroom design • Use carpet squares to designate where the child should sit • The natural environment should support social interaction • Evaluate classroom lighting to determine its effect on child • Create a safe environment that offers protection from teasing and bullying	• Plan individual instruction for content knowledge • Review and determine the most appropriate curriculum for the child's needs • Be prepared to provide follow-up instruction • Provide a consistent classroom schedule and structure • Use simple instructions during lessons • Accept children's responses to questions • Enhance curriculum with the inclusion of social stories	• Encourage and reinforce positive behavior as it is exhibited • Monitor instruction and ask for feedback during lessons • Show a sample of the work that is expected from the child • Provide extended "wait time" for responses from the child • Provide self-monitoring checklists (with pictures or photographs) • Provide additional time for the child to complete his or her work • Use concrete objects as much as possible during instruction and evaluation • Evaluate use of instructional technology based on the individual needs of the child
Attention Deficit/ Hyperactivity Disorder (ADHD)	• Organize seating arrangements and classroom furniture to meet the needs of all children • Provide a highly structured environment (e.g., reduce wide open spaces) • Seat the child near the teacher or peer buddy as necessary • Provide soft background music	• Plan individual instruction for content knowledge • Be prepared to provide follow-up instruction • Consider classwide peer tutoring to support curriculum • Medication usage should be considered in curriculum and instructional planning • Avoid changes in routines and structures without offering a warning • Incorporate behavioral interventions including positive reinforcement	• Encourage and reinforce positive behavior as it is exhibited • Use concrete objects as much as possible during instruction and evaluation • Teach self-monitoring strategies

Table 9. Modifications and Accommodations for Young Children, continued

Disability	Classroom Environment	Curriculum Content	Instruction/Evaluation
Speech and Language Impairments	• Organize seating arrangements and classroom furniture to meet the needs of all children • Seat the child near the teacher or peer buddy as necessary • Verbal participation should be promoted through the classroom design • Provide a language-rich environment	• Plan individual instruction for content knowledge • Instructional content should include social communication skills • Be prepared to provide follow-up instruction • Focus curriculum on both language comprehension and language expression (e.g., receptive and expressive language skills) • Incorporate technology that enhances and supports fluency	• Encourage and reinforce positive behavior as it is exhibited • Provide extended "wait time" for responses from child • Allow many opportunities for the child to use language • Use concrete objects as much as possible during instruction and evaluation • Model appropriate vocalizations throughout the child's daily instruction
Hearing Impairments	• Organize seating arrangements and classroom furniture to meet the needs of all children • Seat the child near the teacher or peer buddy as necessary (this holds especially true if the child is relying on residual hearing) • When planning the environment take into consideration the external stimuli that might impact a child's use of specific technologies such as hearing aids or cochlear implants	• Plan individual instruction for content knowledge • Be prepared to provide follow-up instruction • Consider the need for interpreters when designing instructional content • Plan for instruction using more frequent visual materials • Plan group work with the individual student's needs taken into account	• Encourage and reinforce positive behavior as it is exhibited • Avoid turning your back to the child when speaking to him or her • Embed the use of graphic organizers to assist with instructional organization • Integrate sign language with children throughout the day
Vision Impairments	• Organize seating arrangements and classroom furniture to meet the needs of all children; clear pathways as necessary • Seat the child near the teacher or peer buddy as necessary • Evaluate classroom lighting (e.g., brightness and contrast) to determine its effect on the child • Evaluate the size of images and the student's needs when planning the environment	• Plan individual instruction for content knowledge • Be prepared to provide follow-up instruction • Incorporate orientation and mobility skills into curriculum • Design instruction to include auditory models and hands-on manipulatives	• Encourage and reinforce positive behavior as it is exhibited • Provide an introduction and sequence of events prior to instruction • Instruction and evaluation can be optimized through the use of optical devices or Braille access software • Locate and use books with large print during group presentations • Provide instruction considering perceptual issues • Use concrete objects and sensory materials as much as possible during instruction and evaluation

Table 9. Modifications and Accommodations for Young Children, continued

Disability	Classroom Environment	Curriculum Content	Instruction/Evaluation
Orthopedic Impairments	• Organize seating arrangements and classroom furniture to meet the needs of all children; check for accessibility • Design the environment to overcome architectural barriers • Seat the child near the teacher or peer buddy for additional assistance as needed • Evaluate the environment and make adjustments to furniture, writing utensils, coat racks, and art materials • Lower or secure furniture as necessary • Evaluate the portability of the materials within the environment	• Plan individual instruction for content knowledge • Be prepared to provide follow-up instruction • If deemed necessary, develop a health-care plan that is individualized to meet the student's needs	• Encourage and reinforce positive behavior as it is exhibited • Provide assistive technology devices, bookstands, or switches to facilitate instruction and evaluation • Use concrete objects as much as possible during instruction and evaluation
Developmental Disabilities	• Organize seating arrangements and classroom furniture to meet the needs of all children • Seat the child near the teacher or peer buddy as necessary • Provide soft background music • Be prepared to support the child's activity or assign a peer buddy • Evaluate the environment and make adjustments to furniture, writing utensils, coat racks, and art materials	• Plan individual instruction for content knowledge • Be prepared to provide follow-up instruction • Provide consistent classroom schedule and structure that engages all students • Use concrete objects when conducting mathematics activities • Simplify complexity of expected tasks through task analysis • Offer choices for activities that are limited in number	• Encourage and reinforce positive behavior as it is exhibited • Provide more repetition and examples • Use simple instructions during lessons • Monitor instruction and ask for feedback during lessons • Show a sample of the work that is expected from the child • Provide extended "wait time" for responses from the child • Provide time for the child to complete his or her work • Use concrete objects as much as possible during instruction and evaluation
Traumatic Brain Injury (TBI)	• Organize seating arrangements and classroom furniture to meet the needs of all children (the environment should encourage mobility) • Seat the child near the teacher or peer buddy as necessary • Provide soft background music	• Plan individual instruction for content knowledge, taking into account that the learning and curriculum needs of students with TBI are continuously changing • Be prepared to provide follow-up instruction • If deemed necessary, develop a health-care plan that is individualized to meet the student's needs	• Encourage and reinforce positive behavior as it is exhibited • Use concrete objects as much as possible during instruction and evaluation

From *Successful Inclusion Strategies for Early Childhood Teachers* by C. G. Simpson and L. Warner, 2010, pp. 26–29, Waco, TX: Prufrock Press. Copyright 2010 Prufrock Press. Reprinted with permission.

comprehensive lesson plans, but as time goes on, you will develop your own streamlined process that is more efficient and less time consuming to write. Although you may be teaching in an inclusive classroom, resource classroom, co-taught classroom, or self-contained classroom, or possibly even a combination of these settings, you will still need to develop lesson plans. Lesson plans can be a part of your own documentation to show how you are supporting a student's IEP goals. In addition, you will be noting the accommodations and modifications that you include with each lesson, which can be another self-check to ensure that the IEP is being implemented.

IDEA (1997, 2004), mandated access to the general education curriculum for students with disabilities. The general education curriculum is the explicit curriculum (clearly identified by the district or state) for the majority of students in the school, as defined by the content and performance standards that states have identified (Polloway, Patton, & Serna, 2008). Many school districts provide a grade-level curriculum that teachers are required to use. These curriculum guides have already been aligned with the national and state standards (for those states that have established their own standards; e.g., Virginia's Standards of Learning). Special education teachers have expertise in individual learning strategies, but general education teachers have expertise in the content area curriculum.

You will need to collaborate with general education teachers to ensure that the curriculum standards are addressed in your lesson plans. Many teachers have weekly planning meetings where they meet as grade-level teams. Ask if you can be included in those weekly planning meetings. Typically, they work on weekly and unit lesson plans, so you can make sure that your lesson plans align with each grade-level team. Figure 8 shows the components that should be considered when planning, and Figure 9 is an example of a lesson plan form. Some school districts have their own form that they require teachers to use or the grade-level team may have a form it has developed. If you are a resource teacher and work with a number of students in different grade levels and content areas, you may want to create your lesson plans in a spreadsheet. Whatever form you use, planning lessons should be done on a regular basis and with consistency.

Effective Instruction

As an inclusion teacher, you bring a fresh perspective to today's classroom and are aware of the diverse learning needs that present significant challenges for teaching. Consequently, knowing effective instructional practices is essential for student learning. Consistent with IDEA (2004) and the No Child Left Behind Act (2001), effective instruction has now been defined as those practices that are research based and empirically validated (Boardman, Arguelles, Vaughn, Hughes, & Klingner, 2005). Certain instructional practices

Teachers should consider the following components when planning:
- purpose of the lesson;
- learning objectives;
- length of time to teach the lesson;
- number and sequence of lessons (if you are teaching a unit);
- instructional activities (e.g., reading, assignments, projects, homework);
- assessments (e.g., tests/quizzes, projects, reports, presentations);
- materials needed (e.g., textbooks, art supplies, computers); and
- accommodations or modifications needed.

Figure 8. Planning considerations (deBettencourt & Howard, 2007).

Subject: _____

Class period: _____

Number of students: _____

Title of lesson: _____

State or national standards met: _____

Learner objectives: _____

Teacher instruction (How will you teach the content?): _____
_____

Guided practice (What instructional activities will students engage in for practice?): _____
_____

Independent practice (What instructional activities will the students complete independently?): _____
_____

Materials/equipment needed: _____
_____

Assessment (How will you assess if the students meet the objectives?):
_____
_____

Accommodations or modifications needed: _____

Figure 9. Lesson plan template.

or competencies are strongly related to the achievement of students (deBetten-court & Howard, 2007). Basically, you have to know what to teach and how to teach it, but this can be quite challenging because much of what you teach has to be individualized.

Student Interests

Implementing an interest survey or inventory might prove useful to you when trying to learn about your students and to meet their individual needs. According to Roberts and Inman (2009), "an interest inventory allows you to match topics in a unit to the students most interested in those topics. Regardless of ability level or learning style, those kids will work together exploring an aspect of the lesson they find worthy" (p. 139). Roberts and Inman shared the following example of how one teacher used the interest inventory technique with her primary students:

> A unit on sea animals begins with reading a nonfiction story on jellyfish, followed by having students brainstorm a list of sea animals. After the brainstorming session, they write down their first and second choices of which sea animal they would like to research. Groups are formed based on their choices. Students research in the library and create a report with an illustration. Activities in this unit include reading about the animal, creating a web, writing, and using technology. (p. 139)

Remember that the best way to differentiate according to interests is an interest inventory given at the beginning of a unit of study.

> Finding out what students would choose to do and what experience they have had can be instrumental in planning learning experiences that will be meaningful and motivating. You decide what information would be most useful to you as you assign learning experiences to specific students. (Roberts & Inman, 2009, p. 55)

See Figure 10 for an example of an interest inventory on the Bill of Rights.

Increasing Student Engagement

Each district and state will provide you, as a teacher, with curriculum guides that will give you specific information regarding the curriculum to teach and the order or sequence in which that curriculum should be delivered (instruction) to the students. These curriculum guides, however, will not give you any indication of how to teach the content. As the students enter your classroom, you have to be prepared to engage the students immediately. Research has shown that more learning occurs in classrooms where students are consistently engaged in learning (Mastropieri & Scruggs, 2010). When students are not actively engaged in learning, there is too much time available for behavior problems to occur. Instruction needs to begin once the students arrive in the classroom. This can be done by having some type of warm-up activity planned that prepares them for the content that is going to be taught during the class. For example, in a history class, you may have five key words written on the board that students are responsible for identifying in their textbook and writing a brief sentence about each word. This helps the students get focused on the academic content that you will be teaching.

As you plan out your instruction, you have to consider that the students in your classroom present a wide range of ability levels, but in order to address their academic needs, they have to be on task. This can sometimes be a challenge. deBettencourt and Howard (2007) recommended the following:

- Make instruction relevant and at the student's level of learning.
- Keep eye contact with students during presentations.
- Have all materials for independent seatwork at each student's desk.
- Do not digress from the topic under discussion.
- Keep directions to tasks clear and specific.
- Try not to interrupt your teaching presentation to manage classroom misbehavior.
- Maintain a high success rate.
- Provide substantial amounts of positive feedback. (p. 111)

Classwide Peer Tutoring

One instructional strategy that has been found to increase time spent on task, thus increasing academic engagement, is classwide peer tutoring (Spencer, Scruggs, & Mastropieri, 2003; Spencer, Simpson, & Oatis, 2009). All students within the class are paired to tutor one another. Setting up specific guidelines to use this strategy can be helpful. This strategy moves beyond just pairing students together and assigning them work to complete. See Figure 11 for guidelines for implementing classwide peer tutoring.

The role of the teacher moves away from direct instruction to monitoring the pairs of students and providing academic or behavioral support when needed. Research has shown that peer tutoring can be helpful in addressing diverse learning needs and can be used across content and skill areas (Saddler & Graham, 2005; Spencer, 2006).

Stand Up, Speak Out: A Freedom of Speech Unit
Interest Inventory

The Great American Document
Please check one:

- o I have studied the United States Constitution thoroughly.
- o I have studied the Constitution and would like to study it again.
- o I have never studied the Constitution but would like to.
- o I have never studied the Constitution and am really not that interested in it.

Great Speakers
Circle the speaker that you would most like to investigate during this unit of study. These multimedia explorations will include nonfiction books, articles, video clips, and other various print and nonprint sources. Your exploration will be shared with the rest of the class in a presentation.

	John F. Kennedy	Martin Luther King, Jr.
Speakers:	Inaugural Address, 1961 Famous Line: "And so, my fellow Americans: ask not what your country can do for you—ask what you can do for your country."	I Have a Dream, 1963 Famous Line: "I have a dream that my four children will one day live in a nation where they will not be judged by the color of their skin but by the content of their character."

First Amendment Issues
Study the pamphlets given to you today. Which topic would you most be interested in studying for this unit? Number 1 through 4 below to show your interest (with 1 being the most interested in). If you have had any personal experiences with a First Amendment right that you'd be willing to share, please place a star beside it.

_____ Freedom of Speech
_____ Freedom of Religion
_____ Freedom of Press
_____ Freedom of Assembly

Student Speeches
Please check all that apply:

- o I have researched First Amendment issues.
- o I have studied how to write a speech.
- o I have written a speech.
- o I have presented a speech in front of my classmates before.
- o I have presented a speech for a competition before.

Figure 10. Sample interest inventory. From *Strategies for Differentiating Instruction* (2nd ed.) by J. L. Roberts and T. F. Inman, 2009, p. 57, Waco, TX: Prufrock Press. Copyright 2009 Prufrock Press. Reprinted with permission.

1. Pair students together based on reading levels. By examining their reading scores, you can put a stronger reader with a weaker reader, but you don't want the differences to vary too much. Identify one student as the tutor and one as the tutee.
2. Explain the strategy and teach the implementation procedures.
3. Include specific procedures such as one student (tutor) reading the text aloud while the other student (tutee) follows along. Then, the other student reads the same section.
4. Teach error correction procedures (i.e., how do they correct reading errors with respect?).
5. Model the strategy for the students.
6. Have the students take turns completing the written work that might be involved (e.g., a worksheet, an outline).
7. Demonstrate appropriate ways for the students to give feedback to each other.
8. Guide the students through practice.
9. Let pairs switch roles and practice both roles.
10. Remind them that they are only allowed to talk about the assignment!

Figure 11. Implementation guidelines for classwide peer tutoring.

Cooperative Learning

Another strategy that involves students actively working together is cooperative learning. In cooperative learning, students work together in small groups and work collaboratively to complete academic work. This strategy has been shown to increase academic achievement, improve attitudes toward subject matter, and increase cooperation among students from different ethnic backgrounds (Oortwijn, Boekaerts, & Vedder, 2008).

When planning for cooperative learning, consider the ability level of your students and keep teams small with just three or four students. You will also have to decide how long the groups will be working together. They may complete a long-term project together or you may change your groups more frequently for shorter projects or assignments.

Once you decide on your groups, you will need to assign roles for each member. Obviously, these will vary depending on the assignment and the purpose of the activity. Table 10 is an example of the roles and responsibilities for each member.

As in peer tutoring, your role involves monitoring each of the groups and ensuring that students remain on task, interact appropriately, and that all group members are actively involved in the task.

Table 10
Students' Roles and Responsibilities in a Cooperative Learning Group

Role	Responsibility
Reader	Reads all print instructions and makes sure everyone in the group understands the assignment
Recorder	Records/writes down all of the information needed for the assignment
Runner	Collects all materials needed for the assignment
Task organizer	Compiles all of the information and materials for the assignment and makes sure all members are actively involved

Both peer tutoring and collaborative grouping are cost-effective methods, user-friendly, and keep students actively involved. You can also use these strategies across content areas with groups of students who function at highly varied skill levels. As with any strategy, you need to use variety in the strategies that you use. It is possible to overuse a strategy to the point that it no longer keeps the students engaged.

There are also a number of techniques you can use that are individualized to suit students' learning styles and developmental levels. Using color-coding, number lines, mnemonics, and flip charts are just a few strategies that teachers have found to be effective for many of their students. These also provide some variety to traditional instruction. Remember, setting up your classroom for active engagement increases learning.

Planning for academic instruction as an inclusion teacher requires expertise in both disability areas and best practices and effective instructional strategies. You also have an additional layer of responsibility because you must work with a team to develop IEPs and make sure they are implemented. Your job may require you to be in a number of different classrooms and attend numerous planning meetings. Organization will be key to a successful year for you and your students.

Grading and Homework Policies

As part of academic instruction, students need to know the grading and homework procedures for the class. How is homework graded? What are the policies on homework? What happens if homework is late? How are grades assigned? Are grades accessible by students online? Are there eligibility requirements for students involved with extracurricular activities (e.g., marching band, athletics, drama club)? These are all questions that should be answered prior to the start of the year. In most cases it will be up to you, as the teacher, to decide how homework will be graded, what percentage of the homework is included in the total grade, and what happens if the assignment is late. However, if you are teaching in an inclusive classroom, you will be collaborating with the general education teacher and making these decisions as a team.

Developing classroom policies and procedures prior to the beginning of school and communicating these to your students will minimize problems for you and your students. If some changes need to be made once the semester has begun, make these changes at a semester break if possible. This seems to be an appropriate time because semester grades are usually included on the student's permanent record.

With regard to schools that allow online access to grades, it will be important that you keep your grades current and up-to-date. You do not want students and parents checking grades and getting inaccurate information. This practice will also help students and parents recognize specific problems, and this will give them an opportunity to discuss those problems with you before the semester is over. Grades are very important to students and parents, and you want to be sure that everyone involved understands all of the different components that make up the overall grades.

Attendance

For students to be academically engaged, they have to be in class. All schools have attendance policies, but you will need to have your own set of procedures that students will follow when they are absent. Again, these policies will need to be developed collaboratively if you are in an inclusive classroom. You may want to ask other teachers how they deal with missed classroom instruction and assignments so that you can provide some consistency with policies that may already be in place in other classes. This could make it easier for the student who is absent. Punishing a student for being absent does not benefit anyone. Not allowing a student to make up missed assignments or not giving adequate time to make up the work is punishment. Making sure that students who are absent have an opportunity to make up missed assignments will keep them from falling behind in reaching their instructional goals.

Information regarding grading, homework, and absences should be discussed in class but should also be provided in writing to your students and parents. Some ways to communicate this information include (a) parent's night at school, (b) a letter home to parents explaining all of the details where parents and students must sign that they have read and understand the information, (c) posting the information at the front of the class and discussing it, and (d) providing an occasional reminder to students throughout the year. Clear expectations minimize classroom problems.

Conclusion

Planning academic instruction requires a great deal of planning time in addition to the time spent developing and writing the IEP, meeting with the IEP team, and remaining current on best practices for students with disabilities. Because the IEP includes essential information that has to be addressed within the classroom setting for students with disabilities, it is the responsibility of special education teachers to know what is included in each student's IEP. With so many considerations to be made, special education teachers can feel overwhelmed trying to make sure they are in compliance with everything required for each student. For this reason, collaborating with other teachers who are working with the students you are serving can provide support in planning academic instruction that is individualized for students with disabilities.

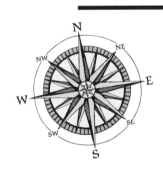

Survival Tips

- Consider establishing a computer spreadsheet at the beginning of the year to help manage student data.

- Warm-up activities can be used to inform instruction through assessing prior knowledge and gauging students' attitudes about the subject matter.

- Strategies that increase student engagement also increase academic performance and learning.

- Set aside a specific time each week to update grades.

Survival Toolkit

Websites to Support You With Accommodations, Modifications, and Curriculum

- Teacher Vision: Inclusion Resources: http://www.teachervision.fen.com/special-education/resource/5346.html

- The Learning Disabilities Association of Texas: Classroom Modifications and Accommodations for Students With Learning Disabilities: http://www.ldat.org/ld_info/accommodations.html

- *Collaborative Teaching: Special Education for Inclusive Classrooms*: Chapter 6: Accommodation Strategies: http://www.parrotpublishing.com/Inclusion_Chapter_6.htm

○ Identifying Accommodations for Inclusion: A Strategy for Special and General Educators: http://www.cehs.wright.edu/~prenick/karen.htm

Books to Support You With Accommodations, Modifications, and Curriculum

Hammeken, P. A. (2000). *Inclusion: 450 strategies for success: A practical guide for all educators who teach students with disabilities* (Rev. ed.). Thousand Oaks, CA: Corwin.

Janney, R., & Snell, M. E. (2004). *Modifying schoolwork* (2nd ed.). Baltimore, MD: Paul H. Brookes.

Pierangelo, R., & Giuliani, G. (2007). *Understanding, developing, and writing effective IEPs: A step-by-step guide for educators*. Thousand Oaks, CA: Corwin Press.

Roffman Shevitz, B., Stemple, M., Barnes-Robinson, L., & Jeweler, S. (2011). *101 school success tools for smart kids with learning difficulties*. Waco, TX: Prufrock Press.

Salend, S. J. (2010). *Creating inclusive classrooms: Effective and reflective practices* (7th ed.). Upper Saddle River, NJ: Pearson/Merrill Prentice Hall.

6 Assessment in the Inclusive Classroom

What is assessment? Why is assessment important? What are different types of assessment? What assessments give the best information to teachers who teach in inclusive classrooms? Why do you need to incorporate assessment into your teaching? These questions, along with others, will be answered in this chapter. Teachers who will be working in inclusive classrooms will need to consider many different factors to become highly efficient and effective teachers. Assessment is one of those factors. Without a clear understanding of how to assess students with varying abilities, you will not know how your students are achieving, nor will you know how you are doing as a teacher. Most teachers think that effective instruction and student learning are the factors they need to focus on; however, if assessment is not addressed the other two factors cannot be determined.

Assessment: Structured and unstructured methods of determining a student's academic interests and social, emotional, or behavioral functioning. Methods include standardized tests, behavioral observations, inventories, rating scales, and interviews.

How will you know if you are an effective teacher? How will you know if your students are learning? How will you know how much progress your students have made during the school year? The use of strong assessment techniques can help teachers in answering these questions. In addition, keeping documentation of student progress, as well as accurate record keeping, can protect you as a teacher. It is very critical for a teacher to keep detailed records when working with students with disabilities in an inclusive classroom. For example, if you served a child a year ago in your classroom and a parent deems a year later that IDEA was violated during the time in which the child received services in the inclusive classroom, you would likely be part of the due process hearing if it occurred. We recommend that you maintain documentation on individual students for just this reason.

This chapter will address the purposes of assessment, formal and informal assessments, performance-based assessments, portfolio assessment, and student self-assessment. Specifically, assessment will be addressed as it relates to teachers who teach in inclusive classrooms. After reading this chapter, you should gain a better understanding of assessment and understand the value assessment holds, develop new ideas about how to use assessment as a tool linked to effective instruction, and feel prepared to address assessment in an inclusive classroom.

✒ **Purposes of Assessment**

There are three main purposes for conducting assessment within an inclusive environment. These include (a) monitoring student progress, (b) making instructional decisions, and (c) evaluating student achievement.

Monitoring Student Progress

Effective teachers are able to determine what students know and what they don't know. They are able to figure out what students understand and what they are having problems with, and are able to infer what might be the cause of the problems. This requires that teachers monitor students' overall progress, not just their individual knowledge of facts and skills. It involves gaining insight into their thinking, not simply knowing whether their answers are right or wrong. This means that teachers need to use assessment to actually figure out why students are making mistakes. Error analysis can help teachers to make this determination. Error analysis is the study of the kind and quantity of errors that occur. For examples, see the following problems.

$$\begin{array}{r} 28 \\ + \underline{37} \\ 65 \end{array} \qquad \begin{array}{r} 45 \\ + \underline{26} \\ 611 \end{array} \qquad \begin{array}{r} 37 \\ + \underline{44} \\ 711 \end{array} \qquad \begin{array}{r} 54 \\ + \underline{18} \\ 72 \end{array} \qquad \begin{array}{r} 88 \\ + \underline{36} \\ 1114 \end{array}$$

correct   incorrect   incorrect   correct   incorrect

Sometimes, the student got this type of problem correct and other times he did not. If the teacher just marked them as correct and incorrect, the student would receive 2/5 correct. Using error analysis the teacher can see that the student got 2/5 correct, but for the three that were incorrect the student did not perform the mathematical operation of carrying properly. Thus, the teacher can either assess the learning more thoroughly or give this student more instruction and practice on carrying.

Making Instructional Decisions

Once teachers have a reasonable understanding of students' knowledge and skill levels, they can use this information to guide teaching practice. Understanding exactly what students know and do not know can help them in making decisions about appropriate content, sequencing and pacing, and modifying activities for particular students. This is particularly important in inclusive classrooms, where the abilities of students may fall across a larger range. This makes instruction responsive to students' needs and should assist students in gaining quality content knowledge and skills.

Teaching practice that is responsive to students' needs uses moment-by-moment assessment to provide information for modifying instruction as it is taking place: deciding whether to continue with a lesson/activity, to adapt or modify it, or to discontinue the instruction all together. Teachers can observe students as they work, question them about what they are learning, and look for other signs that might provide information on how learning is proceeding. Responsive teaching practice also uses more formal assessment strategies such as checklists, journal entries, work samples, exit problems, and quizzes to provide information ahead of time that may be useful for making instructional decisions.

Evaluating Student Achievement

Assessment becomes evaluation when the purpose is to communicate a student's learning to someone who is outside of the classroom (e.g., parents). At regular intervals during the school year, teachers are expected to provide answers to the question, "How does each student's understanding at this time compare with the goals the student was expected to have achieved?" Answering that question entails evaluating students. A teacher may have collected a considerable amount of assessment information on individual students. The assessment tool implemented needs to match the purpose of assessing. From the point of view of evaluation, the information is of little use unless the teacher can communicate it to others in a clear and concise manner. Evaluating student achievement involves compressing a large amount of information into a digestible form that parents, students, and other educators can understand (Layton & Lock, 2008).

Formal and Informal Assessments

Formal Assessments

Formal assessments produce data that support the conclusions made from tests or other measures given to students. We usually refer to these types of tests as *standardized measures*. Although formal assessment measures are not always given by the teachers, it is important to understand formal assessment and be able to link the assessment results to developing effective interventions. A standardized test is administered and scored in a consistent or standard manner. Standardized tests are designed in such a way that the questions, conditions for administering, scoring procedures, and interpretations are consistent and are administered and scored in a predetermined, standard manner (Overton, 2006). These tests produce different types of scores (i.e., overall, clusters, subtests) and compare the scores of the test taker to that of the norm sample that has already taken the test. For example, a fourth-grade student might take a test and then his scores could be compared to other fourth graders who took it. This analysis can tell us if the student is doing better, the same, or worse than students in his same grade. Examples of tests include the KeyMath 3, Woodcock Reading Mastery Tests–Revised, and the Woodcock-Johnson III—Tests of Achievement. Typically, teachers with a background in special education or a school psychologist would administer these types of tests. Scores such as percentiles, stanines, or standard scores are commonly derived from this type of assessment.

Formal or standardized measures should be used to assess overall achievement, to compare a student's performance with others at his or her age or grade level, or to identify strengths and weaknesses compared to peers (Pierangelo & Giuliani, 2006). Formal assessments are the conventional method of testing that we are all very familiar with from our school days. Tests such as the ACT and SAT are classified as formal assessments. These tests are generally used to assess overall achievement, compare a student's performance to that of his peers, or find a student's strengths and weaknesses (Salvia, Ysseldyke, & Bolt, 2007). Formal assessments are further broken down into separate groups: norm-referenced tests and criterion-referenced tests.

Norm-referenced tests. These tests have strict rules in their implementation. Because these tests are used as comparisons between one student and another or one group of students and another group, schools must implement these tests under specific and similar circumstances in each instance of test taking. The advantage of this is that students, parents, and teachers have the advantage of knowing how each student compares to his peers (i.e., students his own age, gender, or grade level). This can give all involved a good look at what needs to be retaught, relearned, or reviewed, as well as showing what lessons and instruction were most effective throughout the learning term.

Another advantage of norm-referenced tests is that, although they are highly specific in implementation, they are easily administered. All of the materials are ready, all of the materials are the same, and because each time taking the test must also be the same, there is little to worry about. Students and teachers alike know what to expect from the test and just how the test will be conducted and graded. Likewise, each and every school will conduct the measure in the same manner, reducing inaccuracies such as time differences or environmental differences that may cause distractions to the students. This also makes these assessments fairly accurate as far as results are concerned, a major advantage for a test (Salvia et al., 2007.)

Yet, to every advantage there are disadvantages, and norm-referenced tests are no different. These tests, like any other, also have distinct disadvantages, including the heavy reliance on multiple-choice questions. If you can remember back to your standardized test days, then you'll recall that many if not all of the questions were multiple choice. This makes it easy on the grader, as she can use a machine to score the tests, but it creates a disadvantage as far as assessment goes. The student is never challenged to come up with the answer himself. He is never charged with specifically remembering the details. As such, the assessment may only measure a broad base of understanding and might not assess the depth of a student's knowledge.

Moreover, these sorts of standards-based assessments measure the level that a student is currently performing at by measuring his score against where his peers are currently performing, instead of the level at which the student should perform (Overton, 2006). Ideally, teachers should measure a student from the standpoint of "This is where the student needs to be, and this is where the student is." However, norm-referenced assessments miss that point and only show how the student compares to other students. Although this is helpful in measuring an individual student, it isn't enough to fully comprehend the student's level of achievement. It isn't enough to fully measure what the child has learned and what he needs to learn in order to reach those essential standards mapped out for each grade level. For gifted students, these types of measures do not show how far above their peers the gifted student has performed. For example, a student earning a score of 100% on a fourth-grade standardized mathematics test may also be able to score at the 90% percentile or above on the same test for fifth graders, meaning that his instruction in mathematics needs to be advanced significantly more than that of his peers. With such a disadvantage as this, it can only measure whether a child is ahead of or behind his peers in his area of testing.

Criterion-referenced tests. These tests help to make up for the lack of specific information on norm-referenced tests. Criterion-referenced tests measure a child's performance and compare it to a standard, instead of to another student ("Formal and informal assessments," 2006). Essentially, these tests are able to actually track or measure a student's mastery of a specific skill, which is ideal for areas such as grammar and mathematics.

An advantage is that criterion-referenced tests are able to measure specific skills a student has and very clearly identify a student's area of mastery. As one skill is tested against a standard, the student is measured against that standard and given an appropriate score. There is no grey area by which to misinterpret the results. The teacher and student are left with a very succinct picture of whether the student has or has not mastered the desired skill.

Furthermore, criterion-referenced tests provide students with very little ambiguity as far as what they are being tested on. Students are made aware of the topics, subjects, or areas they are being tested on beforehand and are, or should be, fully prepared for the exam. The teacher has without a doubt covered the material on the test, unlike other standardized exams that cover a broad range of materials that occasionally have not been taught in a particular classroom. With a criterion-referenced test, students will each be provided with the same advantages, as they have all learned the same material together.

However, students find criterion-referenced tests as some of the most threatening and stressful exams to take ("Formal and informal assessments," 2006). Clearly, the tests put students right out in the open where a failure or low performance can be more readily chastised. Failing can lead to not matriculating to the next grade level or the repetition of an entire concept. With such high stakes, it is no wonder that students feel threatened by taking these sorts of exams. This raises the question of how to deal with students who cannot deal with pressure, as they are more likely to do poorly on an exam of this level than a more casual test.

Likewise, these sorts of tests are developmentally time consuming ("Formal and informal assessments," 2006). Because a specific area must be tested, the test must also be made highly specific. It can take a great deal of time to determine and map out the types of questions and decide which are the most appropriate to measure a student's mastery. As such, it can take a great deal of time before a test is updated or changed, and new students can end up taking the same tests their predecessors took.

Informal Assessments

The second form of assessment is informal assessments, which make up another area of testing that helps teachers to catalogue immediate results from their students. Informal assessments should be used to inform instruction. The most effective teaching is based on identifying performance objectives, instructing according to these objectives, and then assessing these performance objectives. In an inclusive classroom, students with an IEP may work off performance objectives that differ from those of other students in the classroom. Moreover, for any objectives not attained, intervention activities to reteach these objectives need to be developed. Instead of being driven by data, informal assessments are centered on content and performance (Overton, 2006). Because informal assessments make up such a broad and open-ended range of assessments, there are a great number of different possible assessments. Informal assessments aid the teacher by providing quick answers as to the level of learning and understanding attained by a student. Informal assessments are not data driven but rather are content and performance driven. For example, running records are informal assessments because they indicate how well a student is reading a specific book. Scores such as 10 correct out of 15, percentage of words read correctly, and most rubric scores are given from this type of assessment.

Teachers should also consider implementing some type of preassessment with their students. In order to differentiate and match curricula to individual needs, interests, abilities, and levels of readiness, teachers need to find out as much as they can about their students. It is very important to obtain information to document the starting place for students and also to be able to inform parents as to why their children are engaged in the different learning experiences in your classroom. Preassessment information can help justify why different students are doing different types of activities. By collecting preassessment data, instructional strategies can be matched to individual interests and levels of achievement. Preassessment is a critical component of the process if instruction is to be meaningful and motivating to students, as it helps to establish the starting point for learning experiences so students, teachers, and parents can see what progress is being made (Roberts & Inman, 2009). Preassessment helps the teacher to learn what students already know and where instruction can begin.

Preassessment: Provides the teacher with information about what the student knows, understands, and is able to do prior to teaching the unit.

Assessment must be in place to help teachers make informed instructional decisions. Data is obtained to guide instruction and forms the intent of why you're teaching, to whom, and how it will be done. It allows teachers to meet individual student needs with the implementation of differentiated learning experiences. Differentiated learning experiences are essential if *all* of your students are going to make continuous progress (Roberts & Inman, 2009). Although we would like to think all students are in the same place and learn the same way, they do not. Today, especially in an inclusive classroom, teachers need to be aware of the way their students learn and how best to teach them.

Preassessment Strategies

There are various preassessment strategies that will be very beneficial to an inclusion teacher. These strategies provide the teacher with information about what the student knows, understands, and is able to do prior to teaching the unit (Roberts & Inman, 2009). Some examples of strategies that can be implemented include (a) end-of-the-previous-unit assessment, (b) end-of-the-unit assessment, and (c) K-W-L charts.

End-of-the-previous-unit assessment. If the unit you are teaching follows a previous unit and skills are sequential, you will already be prepared for your students as you can use data you already have (Roberts & Inman, 2009). This assessment data can provide you with the information you need to plan learning experiences that match the level of understanding and achievement of both individual students and groups of students in your inclusion classroom. Using classroom data from the unit you just completed can help influence your instructional decisions for the next unit.

End-of-the-unit assessment. End-of-the-unit tests are often employed by teachers to measure students' learning. As a preassessment, if your objectives and the learning focus are clear, then using this type of culminating activity to determine students' prior knowledge should be fine. A student does not need to participate in learning concepts he already has learned or knows. By using the assessment planned for the conclusion of the unit, you provide the opportunity for students to demonstrate what they know, understand, and can do in relation to the unit prior to even beginning it. Without the preassessment, you assume that how well the students do on the end-of-the-unit assessment is a result of your teaching the unit; on the other hand, students may be able to meet all or part of the unit goals before the unit begins, and you weren't even aware of it (Roberts & Inman, 2009).

K-W-L charts. K-W-L charts are a fantastic type of assessment to aide the teacher when starting a unit of instruction. The K is the cue for students to individually tell the teacher what they already know about the topic. The W prompts the students to tell what they want to learn about the topic. Finally, the L encourages students to identify what they want to learn about the topic. Information from the K-W-L chart can guide the teacher to make instructional decisions that directly impact students' learning by motivating them to learn new material and skills directly related to their questions (Roberts & Inman, 2009). You also may actually find some topics you had not considered based on what and how your students say they want to learn.

Examples of two completed K-W-L charts can be seen in Figures 12 and 13. You can see from the charts what Sarah and Alex know about electricity, what they want to learn about the topic, and how they want to go about learning more about it. Each question provides information that will help the teacher plan their instructional unit. Using K-W-L charts as your preassessment also will tell you who has studied the specific content before and who is experiencing it for the first time (Roberts & Inman, 2009).

When Are Assessments Appropriate?

Overall, every assessment, whether formal or informal, has advantages and disadvantages. No assessment is perfect, and many will argue that some forms of assessment contain bias. Additionally, informal and formal assessments, in their various forms, are best when used in conjunction with each other. No one form can provide all of the information a teacher needs. Multiple forms of assessment can provide teachers with the insight they need to pinpoint areas of mastery and areas where students need additional help, while also providing students with data as to their achievements and the kind of help they need to meet the standards laid out by local and government education boards. Assessments are key to education and without them both teachers and students suffer greatly (Overton, 2006).

Examples of Informal Assessments

Writing samples. One example of an informal assessment is a writing sample. Writing samples are advantageous due to the fact that students must apply techniques learned in the classroom to complete this assessment (McMillan, 2007). Very structured assessments make it hard to judge how well students can apply the information they have learned. Instead, a writing sample allows students to write more practically and naturally, and thus allows the teacher to assess how much information the students have grasped and are able to use comfortably. Additionally, a writing sample has the advantage of assessing a number of different concepts. Instead of assessing only one concept, a writing sample can provide outlook on a number of different topics (both current and retrospective). Things such as mechanics, spelling, number of sentences, number of words, and number of paragraphs can be calculated. In essence, it assesses current knowledge along with that previously learned in an effort to test the students on their overall progress and not simply the progress of the current lesson. It is also very important to really know your students. For example, if you have a student with writing difficulties, then a writing sample (an open

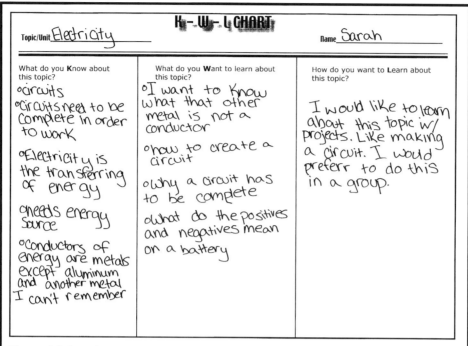

Figure 12. Sarah's completed K-W-L chart. From *Strategies for Differentiating Instruction* (2nd ed.) by J. L. Roberts and T. F. Inman, 2009, p. 51, Waco, TX: Prufrock Press. Copyright 2009 Prufrock Press. Reprinted with permission.

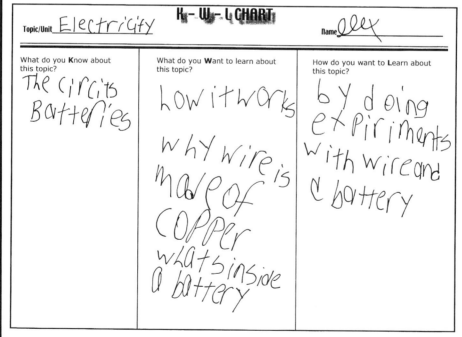

Figure 13. Alex's completed K-W-L chart. From *Strategies for Differentiating Instruction* (2nd ed.) by J. L. Roberts and T. F. Inman, 2009, p. 51, Waco, TX: Prufrock Press. Copyright 2009 Prufrock Press. Reprinted with permission.

prompt with a time limit) could pose serious problems for her. In this case, the writing difficulty combined with the time limit could hinder her performance and thus the assessment would not be an accurate representation of the work the student could achieve. Students with learning difficulties may need accommodations implemented so that they can perform up to their ability. Some examples of accommodations could include typing on the computer, using a tape recorder to record thoughts and then writing them down, planning software to help them get their ideas down on paper, or even making a PowerPoint presentation of their ideas versus writing a full essay.

Homework. Another type of informal assessment is homework. Homework is a great form of assessment and is readily available to any teacher. One reason can be attributed to its timely gathering of information as to which students understood a lesson. Because the lesson is given the same day as the homework, the concepts are not only reviewed, but assessed by doing homework. Furthermore, this type of assessment is often not as time consuming as other forms. It is easily created and implemented and can be as easy to grade as handing it back to the students and reviewing the answers in class. It also gives the teacher data in relationship to the students' learning. If students have done well on the homework, then the teacher can plan to move forward in the curriculum the next day. If the students do poorly, however, then this may warrant stopping to reteach the content, providing more modeling, guidance, direction, and practice the next day.

Debates. Debates are able to assess students' oral skills in a way that other forms of assessment miss. For example, written assessments can hardly test a student's spoken ability, yet a debate is a perfect way for the teacher to see firsthand the kind of progress and achievement a student is making orally. Additionally it provides the teacher a means of seeing how comfortable the student is with speaking aloud in class. Another advantage is that debates require a great deal of organization and understanding of the materials at hand. By holding a debate, a teacher can assess a student on the skills she's used to organize her information and how well she understands that information and combines it into a complete and convincing piece of work. Analyzing debates, however, can be difficult. It would be advised that the teacher have a checklist of what should be included or a rubric that is shared with the students. More information on rubrics will follow later in this chapter.

Experiments. Experiments, another type of informal assessment, can provide a means of shaking up the normal classroom routine and giving students a chance to move around and become part of the lesson. But more than that, experiments can actually provide teachers with insight into how much the students have learned. Experiments allow students a chance to apply, in a very hands-on and practical way, what they have learned. For example, if a student's experiment is successful after a thorough lesson on the concept, it shows that the student has grasped the concept being taught. Additionally, experiments are extremely easy to measure as far as achievement goes. An experiment is very clean cut and a teacher knows what results to expect. Moreover, with lab notes a teacher can easily determine what went wrong and which parts of the lesson the student didn't understand. Appropriate parts of the lesson can either be retaught to the class or corrected in the lab notes so that students have a chance to see how they should have conducted the experiment. Another method of correction can include conducting the same experiment in front of the class; they can take notes and participate for added learning. Experiments, however, can be expensive, as they require a great number of materials, and they can take quite a bit of time to conduct. Sometimes a lab can take the entire class period, or even longer! This makes it hard on teachers, as enough time has to be set aside for the implementation of the assessment.

Performance-Based Assessments

Performance-based assessments are an alternative to traditional methods of testing student achievement. Although traditional testing requires students to answer questions correctly (often on a multiple-choice test), performance-based assessments require students to demonstrate knowledge and skills, including the process by which they solve problems. Performance-based assessments measure skills such as the ability to integrate knowledge across disciplines, contribute to the work of a group, and develop a plan of action when confronted with a new situation. Performance-based assessments are also appropriate for determining if students are achieving the higher standards set by states for all students.

• •

Performance-based assessments: Require students to demonstrate knowledge and skills, including the process by which they solve problems.

• •

Performance-based assessments are sometimes characterized as assessing real life, with students assuming responsibility for self-evaluation. Testing is done to a student, while performance assessment is done by the student as a form of self-reflection and self-assessment. The overriding philosophy of performance-based assessment is that teachers should have access to information that can provide ways to improve achievement, demonstrate exactly what a student does or does not understand, relate learning experiences to instruction, and combine assessment with teaching (emTech, n.d.).

The Office of Technology Assessment of the U.S. Congress (1995) described performance-based assessment as testing that requires a student to create an

Table 11
Examples of Performance-Based Assessments

Assessment	Result
Group project	Enables a number of students to work together on a complex problem that requires planning, research, internal discussion, and group presentation. Final products could be in the form of a paper, webpage, movie, or podcast.
Oral discussion	Assesses students' understanding of a subject through an oral discussion that is very similar to how an academic doctoral candidate would perform a thesis defense.
Real-world simulation	A real-world problem is proposed and students solve the problem based on content learned. Students try to prove they understand the content by solving the given problem. Multiple answers could be possible.
Demonstration	Gives students opportunities to show their mastery of subject-area content and procedures. Students could play an instrument, act out a specific situation, or show others a certain process (e.g., how to do something).
Individual project	In response to a prompt from the teacher, students construct a tangible product that reveals their understanding of certain concepts and skills or their ability to analyze, apply, or evaluate those concepts and skills. This allows individual students to choose a product that interests them. Some examples include the use of technology (e.g., PowerPoint presentation, movie, or podcast), developing a magazine cover, an interactive game, a timeline or a map, and constructing a model.

answer or a product that demonstrates his knowledge or skills. See Table 11 for some examples of performance-based assessments.

One key feature of all performance-based assessments is that they require students to be active participants. They also focus attention on how students arrive at their answers and require them to demonstrate the knowledge or skills needed to obtain a correct answer. For example, if high school juniors are asked to demonstrate their understanding of interest rates by shopping for a used car loan (i.e., comparing the interest rates of banks and other lending agencies and identifying the best deal), a teacher can easily see if the students understand the concept of interest, know how it is calculated, and are able to perform mathematical operations accurately (Project Appleseed, n.d.).

Examples of Performance-Based Assessment

Tasks used in performance-based assessment include essays, oral presentations, open-ended problems, hands-on problems, real-world simulations, and other authentic tasks. Such tasks are concerned with problem solving and understanding. Implementing a variety of assessments is very important for a teacher in an inclusive classroom, as students will exhibit a variety of different learning styles and preferences. Just like standardized achievement tests, some performance-based assessments also have norms, but the approach and philosophy are much different than with traditional standardized tests. The underlying concept is that students should produce evidence of accomplishment of curriculum goals that can be maintained for later use as a collection of evidence to demonstrate achievement and perhaps also the teacher's efforts to educate their students (emTech, n.d.).

Portfolios

A student portfolio is a systematic collection of student work and related material that depicts a student's activities, accomplishments, and achievements in one or more school subjects. A portfolio is not a random collection of observations or student products; it is systematic in that the observations that are noted and the student products that are included relate to major instructional goals. For example, book logs kept by a student over the year can serve as a reflection of the degree to which a student is building positive attitudes and habits with respect to reading. A series of comprehension measures will reflect the extent to which a student can construct meaning from text. Developing positive attitudes and habits and increasing the ability to construct meaning are important outcomes from portfolio use.

Portfolio: Systematic collection of student work and related material that depicts a student's activities, accomplishments, and achievements in one or more school subjects.

The collection should include evidence of student reflection and self-evaluation, guidelines for selecting the portfolio contents, and criteria for judging the quality of the work. The goal is to help a student assemble a portfolio that illustrates her talents, represents her writing capabilities, and tells her stories of school achievement (Venn, 2000). Portfolio assessment ranges from portfolios that demonstrate the student's best work to an "expanded student record" that holds a full representation of the student's work, from math equations to essays on literature. There has been some confusion in the field as to for whom the portfolio is being kept. For example, in some cases, student portfolios serve as a replacement for the high school diploma or transcript. At the elementary and middle school levels, a portfolio can be very beneficial, showing progress (where a student began and how much she has learned and improved) over time. Because a student will be involved in this process (collecting and analyzing her work), she will be better able to understand how she is performing and be able to communicate this information to her parents. Some schools create portfolios that serve as a representative sample of a student's work, showing the range of performance and experience. Other schools want to use portfolios as an assessment tool to provide an alternative to standardized or teacher testing. Through this process a teacher can look at student growth in an academic subject over time.

Why Use a Portfolio?

In this new era of performance-based assessment related to the monitoring of students' mastery of a core curriculum, portfolios can support instructional goals; reflect change and growth over a period of time; encourage student, teacher, and parent reflection; and provide for continuity in education from one year to the next. Instructors can use them for a variety of specific purposes, including (a) encouraging self-directed learning, (b) enlarging the view of what is learned, (c) fostering learning about learning, (d) demonstrating progress toward identified outcomes, (e) creating an intersection for instruction and assessment, (f) providing a way for students to value themselves as learners, (g) offering opportunities for peer-supported growth, and (h) reflecting the complex nature of reading and writing.

Types of Portfolios

Process and product portfolios represent the two major types of portfolios. A process portfolio documents the stages of learning and provides a progressive record of students' growth. A product portfolio demonstrates mastery of a learning task or a set of learning objectives and contains only the best work. Teachers use process portfolios to help students identify learning goals, document progress over time, and demonstrate learning mastery. In general, teachers prefer to use process portfolios because they are ideal for documenting the stages that students go through as they learn and progress (Venn, 2000). Interviews with teachers in inclusive classrooms indicate that portfolios enable them to capture a true picture of students' achievements throughout a specific unit of study.

Steps in the Portfolio Assessment Process

First, the teacher and the students need to clearly identify the portfolio contents, which could include samples of student work, reflections, teacher observations, and conference records. Second, the teacher should develop evaluation procedures for keeping track of the portfolio contents and for grading the portfolio. Third, the teacher needs a plan for holding portfolio conferences, which are formal and informal meetings in which students review their work and discuss their progress. Because they encourage reflective teaching and learning, these conferences are an essential part of the portfolio assessment process (Venn, 2000).

Advantages and Disadvantages of Portfolio Assessment

An important dimension of portfolio assessment is that it should actively involve the students in the process of assessment (McMillan, 2007). By doing so, portfolio assessment has many advantages that include (Venn, 2000):

(a) promoting students' self-evaluation, reflection, and critical thinking;

(b) measuring performance based on genuine samples of students' work;

(c) providing flexibility in measuring how students accomplish their learning goals;

(d) enabling teachers and students to share the responsibility for setting learning goals and for evaluating progress toward meeting those goals;

(e) giving students the opportunity to have extensive input into the learning process;

(f) facilitating cooperative learning activities, including peer evaluation and tutoring, cooperative learning groups, and peer conferencing;

(g) providing a process for structuring learning in stages;

(h) providing opportunities for students and teachers to discuss learning goals and the progress toward those goals in structured and unstructured conferences; and

(i) enabling measurement of multiple dimensions of students' progress by including different types of data and materials.

The disadvantage of portfolios is that they're not as quick and easy to evaluate as traditional assessments. Other disadvantages include (Venn, 2000):

(a) extra time is required to plan for and put together portfolios;

(b) the gathering of all the necessary data and work samples can make portfolios bulky and difficult to manage;

(c) developing a systematic and deliberate management system is difficult, but this step is necessary in order to make portfolios more than a random collection of student work;

(d) scoring portfolios involves the extensive use of subjective evaluation procedures such as rating scales and professional judgment, and this limits reliability; and

(e) scheduling individual portfolio conferences is difficult and the length of each conference may interfere with other instructional activities.

Implications of Portfolio Use

There are many implications for teachers who implement portfolios. First, some people believe that using portfolios will enable teachers to broaden their curriculum to include areas they traditionally could not assess with standardized testing. How well this works depends on how much a curriculum is developed "to the test"; in other words, how much curriculum is geared toward achieving high test scores rather than learning for learning's sake. Second, portfolio assessment appears to complement a teacher's use of instructional strategies centered around teamwork, projects, and applied learning. Portfolios are also compatible with more individualized instruction, as well as strategies focused on different learning styles. Teachers can also utilize portfolios to judge student performance. Plus, students can use their own portfolios for self-assessment and reflection (Funderstanding, n.d.).

Data Collected

There are many ways in which portfolios have proven effective. They provide teachers with a wealth of information upon which to base instructional decisions and from which to evaluate student progress (Dotson & Henderson, 2009). They are also an effective means of communicating students' developmental status and progress in reading and writing to parents (Romeo, 2008). Teachers can use their record of observations and the collection of student work to support the conclusions they draw when reporting to parents. Portfolios can also serve to motivate students and promote students' self-assessment and self-understanding (Gearhart & Osmundson, 2009). Lopez (2002) indicated that major dimensions of an expanded concept of validity are consequences, fairness, transfer and generalizability, cognitive complexity, content quality, content coverage, meaningfulness, and cost efficiency. Portfolios are an especially promising approach to addressing all of these criteria.

Portfolios are an effective way to bring assessment into harmony with instructional goals. Teachers determine important instructional goals and how they might be achieved. Through observation during instruction and collecting some of the artifacts of instruction, assessment flows directly from the instruction (Gearhart & Osmundson, 2009). Portfolios can contextualize and provide a basis for challenging formal test results based on testing that is not authentic or reliable. All too often, students are judged on the basis of a single test score from a test of questionable worth (Romeo, 2008). Student performance on such tests can show day-to-day variation. However, such scores diminish in importance when contrasted with the multiple measures of reading and writing that are part of a literacy portfolio.

Self-Assessment

Self-assessment is the most overlooked, yet possibly most valuable, aspect of assessment for students at all levels and in all fields. Self-evaluation is defined as students judging the quality of their work, based on evidence and explicit criteria, for the purpose of doing better work in the future. When we teach students how to assess their own progress, and when they do so against known and challenging quality standards, we find that there is a lot to gain. Self-evaluation is a potentially powerful technique because of its impact on student performance through enhanced self-efficacy and increased intrinsic motivation. Evidence about the positive effect of self-evaluation on student performance is particularly convincing for difficult tasks, especially in academically oriented schools and among high-need pupils. Perhaps just as important, students like to evaluate their work (Rolheiser & Ross, n.d.). Such self-assessment encourages students to become independent learners and can increase their motivation (National Capital Language Resource Center, n.d.).

• •

Self-assessment: Students judging the quality of their work, based on evidence and explicit criteria, for the purpose of doing better work in the future.

• •

Reasons for Self-Assessment

There are many reasons to implement self-assessment with your students. First, it helps to make students active partners. Second, it involves them in the assessment and evaluation process, which is an essential part of balanced assessment. When students become partners in the learning process, they gain a better sense of themselves as readers, writers, and thinkers. As students reflect on what they have learned and on how they learn, they develop the tools to become more effective learners. Third, students need to examine their work and think about what they do well and in which areas they still need help. To guide students in understanding the process of self-evaluation, you may want to have them complete a self-reflection/self-assessment sheet that you develop. Fourth, once students have reflected on their learning, they are ready to set new goals for themselves. As they work toward these goals, they should be encouraged to reflect on their learning journey at regular intervals. You might have students record their observations during these periods of self-reflection to help reaffirm their goals and motivate them to move toward meeting each goal. With practice, students who self-assess become more conscious learners and are able to apply knowledge of their learning needs and styles to new areas of study. Finally, as students become more active participants in the assessment process, they will begin to evaluate their strengths and attitudes, analyze their progress in a particular area, and set goals for future learning (National Capital Language Resource Center, n.d.).

Self-Assessment Opportunities

Meaningful reflection takes practice. This is as true for students as it is for teachers. You can best support your students in their efforts at self-assessment by providing regular, uninterrupted time for students to think about their progress. At first, you may need to guide their reflection with questions such as these: (a) What did I learn today?, (b) What did I do well?, (c) What am I confused about?, (d) What do I need help with?, (e) What do I want to know more about?, and (f) What am I going to work on next? As students participate in the self-assessment process, they will have many opportunities to collect pieces of their writing and react to things they have read. Individual student conferences can help guide these periods of self-reflection and reinforce the idea that collecting and evaluating work are important steps in self-assessment. Self-assessment can take many forms, including:

- writing conferences,
- discussion (whole-class or small-group),
- reflection logs,
- weekly self-evaluations,
- self-assessment checklists and inventories, and
- teacher-student interviews.

These types of self-assessment share a common theme: They ask students to review their work to determine what they have learned and what areas of confusion still exist. Although each method differs slightly, all should include enough time for students to thoughtfully consider and evaluate their progress.

When students understand the criteria that are needed to meet the teacher's expectations for an assignment or project before they begin the activity, they are more likely to meet those criteria. The key to this understanding is to make the criteria clear. As students evaluate their work, you may want them to set up their own criteria for acceptable and exemplary work. Help them with the clarity of their criteria as they assess their own work. Students' observations and reflections can also provide valuable feedback for refining your instructional plan. As your students answer questions about their learning and the strategies they use, think about their responses to find out what they are really learning and to see if they are learning what you are teaching them. It is important to remember that, in an inclusive setting, some students may have different performance goals based on the IEP objectives. Be sure that the rubric used takes into account the specific needs and expectations of students with IEPs.

Rubrics

A rubric is an evaluation tool that describes the criteria for performance at various levels using demonstrative verbs. It is a performance-based assessment process that accurately reflects content skills, process skills, work habits, and learning results. Rubrics do many things including:

- creating a common framework and language for evaluation;
- providing students with clear expectations about what will be assessed as well as standards that should be met (sending messages about what is most meaningful);
- increasing the consistency and objectivity of evaluating (especially scoring or rating) performances, products, and student understanding;
- providing students with information about where they are in relation to where they need to be for success;
- identifying what's most important to focus on in instruction; and
- giving students guidance in evaluating and improving their work. Students can learn how to think about evaluation. Using rubrics focuses both students and teachers on two essential questions: "What do we want students to know and do?" and "What would exemplary demonstration of this learning look like?"

· ·

Rubric: An evaluation tool that describes the criteria for performance at various levels using demonstrative verbs.

· ·

Types

There are generally two types of rubrics: holistic and analytic. It is important to analyze the task, activity, or project being assessed and determine which type of rubric is most appropriate to apply. A holistic rubric describes a student's work as a single score—the report or project as a whole is assigned a score. Therefore, holistic rubrics are best suited to tasks that can be performed or evaluated as a whole and/or those that may not require extensive feedback. Analytic rubrics specify criteria to be assessed at each performance level, provide a separate score for each criterion, and may include a composite score for overall performance. In some cases, the composite score is weighted based on the importance of each dimension.

Holistic rubrics. These involve one global, holistic rating. They give a single score or rating for an entire product or performance based on an overall impression of a student's work. In essence, one combines all of the important ingredients of a performance or product to arrive at an overall, single judgment of quality. Holistic rubrics are usually more useful for summative and/or large-scale assessment where an overall performance rating is needed. For example, portfolios are often assessed using holistic rubrics.

Analytical rubrics. These divide a product or performance into essential traits or dimensions so that they can be judged separately. A separate score is provided for each trait, resulting in more detailed analysis than is provided by holistic rubrics. Analytical rubrics are usually better for day-to-day classroom use because they provide more detailed and precise feedback to the student. Rubrics are explicit schemes for classifying products or behaviors into categories that vary along a continuum. They can be used to classify virtually any product or behavior such as essays, research reports, oral presentations, and group activities. Assessment data frequently are based on analyzing student products or behaviors. Scoring rubrics are versatile tools for simplifying this review by clearly specifying assessment criteria.

Using rubrics is a way of ensuring that students, teachers, and parents alike know the purpose of the work that students are being asked to do. The use of rubrics as a tool for scoring work has the potential for giving students the power and responsibility that goes with knowing what is being asked of them and how to achieve it.

How Do You Develop a Rubric?

At first, developing rubrics can be difficult. The greatest challenge is for teachers and, ultimately, students, to translate the performance of various assignments to the rubric fairly and reliably. For this they need support, time, and practice. See Figure 14 for the steps to creating a rubric.

Uses

Rubrics have many uses. Rubrics can be integrated into courses by allowing teachers to communicate expectations, provide formative feedback, and grade and assess students. For example, points can be assigned and used for grading, and categories such as beginning, developing, accomplished, and exemplary can be used for assessment. Teachers who share an assessment rubric might assign points in different ways, depending on the nature of their courses, and they might decide to add more rows for course-specific criteria or comments, but the basic concept is the same. We suggest teachers collaborate to come up with a rubric that is easy to understand by both teachers and students. For example, a writing rubric might address the following components that students need to

1. Identify what type of rubric you want to create—holistic or analytic.
2. Identify what learning objective/outcome you are assessing (e.g., critical thinking, oral communication).
3. Identify the characteristics/competencies of the outcome you are assessing.
4. Determine how many levels you will have on your rubric. For example, will you have a level for each grade range (e.g., A-range, B-range, C-range) or will you have only several levels such as "outstanding," "acceptable," and "not acceptable"?
5. Determine a descriptive label for each of these categories. For example, "A-Range" is a category. However, you don't have to use grades. Descriptive words like "Emerging" or "Developing" can sometimes work better as labels for categories because they focus students on the description rather than the grade.
6. Describe the best work you could expect using the characteristics you selected. This describes the top category. The best way to do this is to start with student work that you have sorted into several piles (e.g., excellent, okay, poor). Then read through the excellent pile of work and describe what makes it excellent. This will help you form this top category.
7. Describe the worst acceptable product using the characteristics you selected. This describes the lowest acceptable category. Again, you can do this by starting with the student work and working backward into the language to describe the work in this category.
8. Develop descriptions of intermediate-level products and assign them to intermediate categories. You might develop a scale that runs from 1 to 5 (e.g., unacceptable, marginal, acceptable, good, outstanding), 1 to 3 (e.g., novice, competent, exemplary), or any other set that is meaningful. Use student work to help you determine these levels.
9. Continue to monitor the language and vocabulary you use in your rubric. Make sure it is written in a way your audience will understand.
10. Remember to use sample rubrics for language that you can adopt for your own rubric.
11. Plan to revise your rubric after testing it on student work. Often you will begin with a rubric that seems perfect, but during the process of using that rubric to score student work, you will find areas that you forgot to include on the rubric or that are inadequate and need to be revised.
12. Peer feedback can also help you further revise your rubric.

Figure 14. Steps to creating a rubric.

address in their writing: (a) topic, (b) organization, (c) paragraphs, (d) sentences, (e) vocabulary, (f) grammar, (g) punctuation, (h) spelling, and (i) handwriting (see http://www.teachervision.fen.com/writing/printable/6313.html for a more detailed example). With the use of this rubric, expectations would be clear as to what students need to include in their writing and how they will be assessed for each component.

Complex products or behaviors can also be examined efficiently. We know teachers have many demands on their time, and assessment activities should be structured to use that time effectively. Rubrics focus raters on the learning objectives being assessed, allowing them to tune out extraneous variables. For example, if teachers are analyzing written papers to assess students' ability to synthesize a set of readings, the rubric should help them ignore other aspects of the writing such as personal thoughts, comments, or unrelated information. Well-trained reviewers apply the same, agreed-upon standards to the products being reviewed. This generates data that are likely to be reliable and valid. Summaries of results reveal patterns of students' strengths and areas of concern. These assessments allow us to identify learning objectives that require increased attention. Rubrics are criterion-referenced, rather than norm-referenced. Raters ask, "Did the student meet the criteria for level 5 of the rubric?" rather than, "How well did this student do compared to other students?" This is important for program assessment because you want to learn how well students have met your standards.

SURVIVAL SECRETS OF TEACHERS

Jared, Elementary School Special Education Teacher

What Is Your Current Position and How Long Have You Been Teaching?

I am currently teaching second-, third-, and fourth-grade students in a resource room setting. I often work with other teachers co-teaching in the areas of math and science. I have been teaching for 4 years.

What Were Some of the Issues You Faced With Assessment as a First-Year Teacher?

There were a number of issues that I faced. The first was that my school was tied to standardized assessments. Even though the information gleaned from these assessments didn't really help me or other teachers, that was the situation. Over time I was finally able to show the administration that these assessments were not capable of telling us where in the curriculum the student was or what he or she knew or didn't know. We were spending a lot of time conducting assessments that were not giving us the information that we wanted or needed. Another issue was that I was the decision maker. I stepped into my school as a first-year teacher and was immediately thrust into the role of organizing and conducting assessments. It was a bit overwhelming to me, but after I realized that I knew the content, I became more comfortable with my role. I looked at each situation individually and made a specific assessment decision based on the facts and what was wanted or needed. The last issue I faced was that of proper assessment. It seemed that every student was recommended to take the same assessments. There was no individualization at all. If there was a reading issue it would be the Woodcock Reading Mastery Test-Revised. A math issue was the KeyMath-Revised and so on. I worked very hard to teach school personnel that every assessment decision should be unique to the student and serve the purpose of obtaining the needed results and information. It was not an easy year, but overall much progress was made in the area of assessment throughout the year.

How Did You Communicate Results to Parents and Other Teachers?

Communicating assessment results to parents and other teachers was extremely important for me as a first-year teacher. I needed to make sure that all people involved with a particular student understood what the data meant. Many times at the beginning of the school year I could tell (by the looks on their faces) that participants were unclear or did not understand the data I was presenting. I usually presented the data in an oral report. I quickly changed the way I did things by printing the assessment data on a sheet of paper and handing it to the participants. I also created charts and graphs to actually show the participants how the student performed. Over the course of the school year I could show progress, or lack of it, on these graphs. This information also allowed parents and teachers to be more open to asking questions that got them more involved with the assessment process.

What Advice Would You Give Future Teachers About Assessment?

Assessment is a complicated topic. I would tell future teachers to use their heads and make educated decisions as to what type of assessment they are going to implement. What is the purpose of your assessment? Is it to identify a student? Is it to look at knowledge of a content area? Is it to monitor progress? There are many different types of assessment and each serves its own purpose. Look at the task and what you want to assess. Then develop an assessment that matches your instruction. If students were working in a hands-on environment, then maybe a project-based assessment would work best. If you were teaching factual information, then maybe some type of recall assessment could be used (e.g., matching, multiple choice, definitions). You are the decision maker when it comes to the assessment of your students. Choose something that will give you relevant and useful information.

Conclusion

As a teacher in an inclusive classroom, assessment is instrumental in documenting where students are and what they have learned. In order for your students to experience continuous progress in their learning, you must think about assessment differently. Assessment needs to be authentic and linked to the real world, it should be ongoing throughout a unit (remember that it's not just an ending to the unit), instruction should be a response to assessment, and all students learn differently and may need to be assessed differently.

Assessment in today's inclusive classrooms is very important for teachers to understand. Without assessment you will not know how your students are achieving, nor will you know how you are doing as a teacher. Not only is assessment important, but so is choosing the appropriate assessment for a given situation. By doing so, teachers can obtain accurate data on students to make the most educated decisions possible regarding instruction and how students are performing.

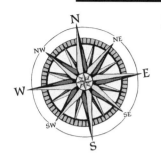

Survival Tips

- Assessment is an ongoing process that should inform instructional decisions.

- Frequently providing parents with assessment data keeps them current on how their child is progressing both academically and behaviorally. That way, there are no surprises when progress reports are mailed home.

- Your colleagues can provide valuable information on which assessments to use and what measures they use to collect data.

Survival Toolkit

Websites to Support You With Assessment

- Assessment Advice & Forms: http://www.teachervision.fen.com/ assessment/resource/5815.html

- Rubrics for Teachers: http://www.rubrics4teachers.com

- Assessment Strategies for Differentiated Instruction: http://boe. ming.k12.wv.us/teachers/di/di_rubrics/introduction%20to%20DI%20 assessment.htm

- Online Resources for Assessment: http://www.rmcdenver.com/ useguide/assessme/online.htm

- Reflective Teaching and Self Evaluation: http://www.sabine.k12. la.us/vrschool/assessment.htm

- Alaska Department of Education & Early Development: A Collection of Assessment Strategies: http://www.eed.state.ak.us/tls/ frameworks/mathsci/ms5_2as1.htm

Books to Support You With Assessment

Herrera, S. G., Murry, K. G., & Cabral, R. M. M. (2007). *Assessment accommodations for classroom teachers of culturally and linguistically diverse students*. Boston, MA: Allyn & Bacon.

Hosp, M. K., Hosp, J. L., & Howell, K. W. (2007). *The ABCs of CBM: A practical guide to curriculum-based measurement*. New York, NY: Guilford Press.

Karnes, F. A., & Stephens, K. R. (2009). *The ultimate guide to student product development and evaluation* (2nd ed.). Waco, TX: Prufrock Press.

Popham, W. J. (2010). *Classroom assessment: What teachers need to know* (6th ed.). Boston, MA: Pearson.

Roberts, J. L., & Inman, T. F. (2009). *Assessing differentiated student products: A protocol for development and evaluation.* Waco, TX: Prufrock Press.

Salvia, J., Ysseldyke, J. E., & Bolt, S. (2009). *Assessment in special and inclusive education* (11th ed.). Belmont, CA: Wadsworth/Cencage Learning.

Spinelli, C. G. (2011). *Linking assessment to instructional strategies: A guide for teachers.* Boston, MA: Pearson.

7 Classroom Management

Effectively managing students' behavior is a critical issue in today's schools. Negative or unacceptable behavior can actually be detrimental to the learning environment and the social development of students. Some schools have a no tolerance policy where certain behaviors constitute an immediate suspension. Some schools have schoolwide behavior policies, while still others leave it up to the classroom teacher. This can cause problems for students, as every teacher has a different set of rules and classroom expectations. As a teacher in an inclusive setting, it will be important for you to understand what the policies are in your school. It will also be important that you educate all of your students so that they understand the behavior policies and what is expected of them in each of their classes.

One of the more challenging areas for teachers, both in special education and general education, is classroom management. This may come as a surprise to new teachers, because teacher education programs often provide training in this area. Thus, why wouldn't new teachers assume that they have learned all they need to know about behavioral issues upon arriving in their classrooms? Recent legislation, such as No Child Left Behind (2001) and IDEA (2004), has brought about changes in our schools that have expanded the diversity of the general education classroom. Too often, we are still working with new teachers who are surprised at the varying levels of academic and behavioral functioning that is seen in most classrooms. Based on a review of the literature, teachers have historically ranked classroom management as being one of their major concerns (Meinick & Meister, 2008; Ritter & Hancock, 2007).

Nearly all classrooms are going to have students who display inappropriate and disruptive behaviors. It is imperative that all teachers are prepared to deal with behavioral issues, but that can only come to fruition if we do a better job at preparing teachers of the realities of the classroom. Table 12 lists the most commonly reported discipline concerns indicated by teachers. "Even though most of these are not serious, 85% of teachers reported that as a new teacher, they felt completely unprepared to deal with student behaviors" (Cihak & Bowlin, 2010, p.112). Many of these behaviors can be easily prevented with the use of effective classroom management skills, the main focus of this chapter.

Motivation and Management

One of the most important steps in effective classroom management is establishing and maintaining a positive, supportive classroom atmosphere. Research has shown that teachers who are the most effective in managing classroom behavior are also usually the most effective in improving classroom achievement (Mastropieri & Scruggs, 2010). Careful planning of instruction will decrease or prevent some of the behavior problems. When students arrive in your classroom, it is important to be well prepared, organized, and positive about what you will be working on in class that day. As a new teacher, you have to be knowledgeable that the manner in which you teach and respond to behaviors can contribute to behavior problems. Kauffman, Mostert, Trent, and Pullen (2006) recommended using the acronym CLOCS-RAM to assist teachers in remembering the characteristics of best instructional practices. These include:

- *Clarity.* Students must know exactly what to do.
- *Level.* Students must be able to do the task with a high degree of accuracy.
- *Opportunities.* Students must have frequent opportunities to respond.
- *Consequences.* Students must receive a meaningful reward for correct performance.
- *Sequence.* The tasks must be presented in logical sequence so that students get the big idea.
- *Relevance.* The task should be relevant to the students' lives, and if possible, the students should understand how and why it is useful.
- *Application.* The teacher helps the students learn how to learn and remember by teaching memory and learning strategies and applying the knowledge and skills to everyday problems.
- *Monitoring.* The teacher continuously monitors students' progress.

In a well-managed classroom, the teacher uses methods and strategies that engage students in active learning. This may include having students work on

Table 12
Most Frequently Reported Discipline Problems

Discipline problem	Percentage of teachers who say the behavior is a "very" or "somewhat" serious problem (%)
Disrupting class by talking	69
Treating teachers with a lack of respect	60
Cheating	58
Showing up late to class	57
Bullying and harassment	55
Rowdiness in common areas such as hallways and lunchroom	51
Truancy and cutting class	45
Illegal drugs	41
Physical fighting	36

Note: From Cihak & Bowlin (2010).

projects in cooperative learning groups, complete tasks with a peer, develop and give presentations, or complete graphic organizers using programs such as Inspiration. Students are more likely to work hard when you vary activities and avoid tediousness and similarity in assignments.

Preventing Behavior Problems

There are also some very simple ways to control potential behavior problems. Using proximity control involves moving closer to students who may be exhibiting some minor disruptive behaviors. Teachers who sit at their desks instead of being up and involved with the students cannot really gauge what is going on in the classroom. Moving around the classroom and assisting or encouraging students as they work can minimize problems and provide a supportive environment for everyone.

Establishing Classroom Rules and Procedures

Rules are key to effective classroom management and are used to prevent behavior problems from occurring. They provide students with the expectations for appropriate classroom behavior. The development of effective rules should involve the students. Students are more likely to follow rules if they have a say in their development, which should include:

1. Discussing the value of rules with the students.
2. Asking for student input to develop rules.
3. Choosing three to five rules written positively.
4. Using simple language.
5. Making sure class rules are consistent with schoolwide rules.
6. Posting the rules in the classroom.
7. Teaching the rules.
8. Implementing the rules consistently.

With only three to five rules, students should be able to remember them. It is also important to use simple language, and make sure the rules are stated positively. For example, instead of saying "No running in the hall," write the rule as, "Walk in the hall." Telling students what *not to do* does not tell them what *to do*. You should not assume that students already know what to do.

Recognizing the importance of developing classrooms rules is a necessity in preventing behavior problems, but equally as important is the teaching of procedures. Procedures are methods for completing class activities and tasks. Classrooms run more smoothly if there are procedures for what we want the students to do, from asking for help, turning in assignments, completing group work, responding to questions, and entering and leaving the classroom.

During the first week of school, it will be necessary to teach those procedures to the students, so you need to think about what you want the students to accomplish while in your classroom. You can use the checklist in Table 13 to help you identify those tasks.

After you have determined what procedures are needed, break down each procedure into steps so that you can explicitly teach these to the students. This may include class discussion, modeling, role-playing, and practice. You can also expect students to need reminders throughout the school year.

Self-Monitoring

Self-monitoring is another successful strategy that can help students who have difficulty staying on task. Increasing on-task behavior reduces the opportunity for behavior problems. Self-monitoring encourages students to be conscious of their own behaviors, keep track of the occurrences of the behaviors, and reward themselves for improvements (Ganz, 2008). Teaching students to self-monitor requires little training. The materials needed are teacher made and specific to each student's needs. The steps for implementing self-monitoring in the classroom include:

- choosing a target behavior;

Table 13
Classroom Procedures Checklist

Classroom procedure	Taught to students?
Entering and exiting the classroom	
Going to/returning from the bathroom	
Responding to questions	
Turning in homework or in-class assignments	
Putting away personal items (e.g., book bags, lunchboxes, coats)	
Using lockers	
Making up homework	
Grading work (including late work)	
Other	

- talking with the student about the advantages of self-monitoring;
- determining how to measure the behavior (e.g., checklist, card);
- teaching the student to self-monitor;
- beginning self-monitoring with the student; and
- fading teacher monitoring.

Self-monitoring: Involves the student monitoring his or her own progress in the effort to develop a skill or complete a project.

Table 14 shows an example of a self-monitoring card. Each student's card will include his own behavioral goals. This particular card was developed so the student can use the same card as he moves from class to class. The teacher can also develop a reward system to use for the student based on how successful he is with the behaviors he is charting.

Classwide Positive Behavior Supports

Research literature over the past decade has provided numerous examples of effective teaching strategies that can help teachers address problem behaviors in the classroom. These strategies include examining the antecedents (i.e., environmental factors that are likely to increase a behavior) and the consequences (i.e., environmental factors that are maintaining the behaviors). Unfortunately, teacher training programs in special education are often limited in teaching

Table 14
Sample Behavior Self-Monitoring Card

Class Period	Expectations (Place a check mark by the completed activities.)
1. Physical Education	_____ Be on time. _____ Change clothes. _____ Begin activity when instructed. _____ Promptly quit the activity when instructed.
2. Band	_____ Be on time. _____ Bring your instrument and practice book. _____ Follow directions.
3. Math	_____ Be on time. _____ Bring your math book, paper, and pencil. _____ Turn in completed homework in folder on teacher's desk. _____ Work quietly on in-class assignment. _____ Raise your hand for teacher assistance.
4. Social Studies	_____ Be on time. _____ Bring social studies book, paper, and pencil. _____ Sit in your assigned seat. _____ Work quietly unless working in a group setting.
5. Study Hall	_____ Be on time. _____ Bring unfinished assignments.
6. Science	_____ Be on time. _____ Bring science book, paper, and pencil. _____ Follow teacher instructions. _____ Talk to your group partner only about the science experiment or activity.
7. Language Arts	_____ Be on time. _____ Bring notebook and pencils. _____ Talk to your group partner only about the language arts project.

these skills. Positive behavior supports (PBS) is a research-based strategy used to promote and reinforce social and behavioral competence in students while minimizing problem behaviors (Farmer et al., 2006). In a PBS classroom, the teacher establishes a structure that is conducive to learning and limits disruptive behaviors. Features of effective classrooms typically include (a) well-designed physical environments, (b) clearly articulated rules and routines, (c) appropriate and effective instruction, (d) reinforcement for positive behaviors, (e) consistent consequences to deter problem behaviors, and (f) teaching of pro-social competencies that allow students to function effectively in the classroom (Cihak & Bowlin, 2010).

• •

Positive behavior supports (PBS): A research-based strategy used to promote and reinforce social and behavioral competence in students while minimizing problem behaviors (Farmer et al., 2006).

• •

PBS has yielded positive results in helping students with behavioral problems adapt to general education classrooms. These supports include a combination of effective behavior management practices, such as positive reinforcement or contingent praise and consistency, in the implementation of classroom rules.

Positive reinforcement refers to the supplying of a desirable consequence after an appropriate behavior. Typically, teachers use positive reinforcement that falls into three categories: social reinforcers (praise), tangible reinforcers, or activity reinforcers. Praise is the easiest to use and can be simply a smile, thumbs-up sign, "Good job," or "Thank you." Although most teachers are well aware of the positive impact that praise can have on student performance, it is frequently underused (Conroy, Sutherland, Snyder, & Marsh, 2008). Praise is a proven generalized reinforcer that increases social and behavioral competence in students (Sutherland, 2000). In order to gain the most benefits, teachers need to specify the target behavior that is being praised (e.g., "Good, you completed all of your math problems."). Praise is also contingent when you use it as a consequence for a specific expected behavior such as following directions or remaining seated during class.

• •

Positive reinforcement: Supplying of a desirable consequence after an appropriate behavior.

• •

The second and third types of reinforcement will involve developing a menu of reinforcer preferences—things that are reinforcing to the individual student (or the entire class). The menu could include tangible items, such as a sticker or something from a prize box, or an activity, such as computer time or free time. The following techniques can be used to develop a menu of reinforcers:

- direct questioning of the student;
- questioning of parents or past teachers;
- observation of the student within the classroom;
- structured observation (i.e., arranging specific reinforcement alternatives for selection); and
- trial and error of a variety of reinforcers.

Next, you have to decide what type of schedule of reinforcement to use when presenting the reinforcer to the student. With a continuous schedule, the reinforcer is given with each occurrence of the target behavior. This type of schedule is most useful for teaching and learning at the acquisition stage. With an intermittent schedule, the reinforcer is given less frequently and increases the chance of maintenance and generalized learning. You need to choose your reinforcement schedule according to the instructional objectives. For example, if you are teaching in-seat behavior, you may want to use a continuous schedule of reinforcement, but once the student has consistently performed that behavior, you can move to an intermittent schedule that will encourage maintenance.

Classwide Token Economy

Another systematic method for programming reinforcement is through a classwide token economy system that provides classroom structure and controls for a variety of distracting and disruptive behaviors. It requires careful planning and some possible trial and error, but it is easy to use and can be very effective. Token economy systems involve the use of tokens (e.g., points, play money, tickets, plastic chips) to reward students for performing expected behaviors that are then exchanged for student-desired items or additional reinforcers such as computer time, books, or free time. When using a token economy reward system, you have to make sure that students understand the connection between the rewards and their behavior. This can be a very effective system and be highly motivating for increasing appropriate classroom behaviors.

In preparing to use this system, you will need to post classroom rules, provide a positive classroom environment, and have the appropriate teaching methods and curriculum materials (Conroy et al., 2008). Table 15 shows a sample of appropriate classroom behaviors and the allotted points. You can individualize the behaviors and point system to support the needs of your own classroom. Bonus points allow the teacher to award extra points to students who exhibit helping behaviors and continuously perform well on the point system.

Because there are always those students who will save up all of their tokens just to announce that they have the most, there should be a forced spending rule that will prevent this from occurring. For instance, students may have to spend all of their tokens at the end of each week. As part of the classwide token economy system, you also will need to establish fines for violations of classroom rules. The fines need to be moderate so that students will not go into debt trying to pay the fines. Once they lose all of their tokens, they are forced out of the classwide system and you lose your leverage. You can always give the students opportunities to earn back points so that they remain in your system.

Once you begin implementing the system, you may have to make some minor changes or adjustments to increase its effectiveness. This system is a

Table 15
Sample Classroom Behaviors and Point System

Behavior	Points earned
Arriving to class on time	3
Having materials for class	3
Following directions promptly	3
Completing work on time	4
Turning in homework	4

positive way to encourage all students to behave appropriately, but it does take commitment from the teacher.

This chapter covers many additional strategies that can be implemented classwide to support positive behaviors within the classroom. In addition, the authors recognize that a majority of classroom management concerns expressed by teachers is disruption of classwide instruction due to students who exhibit attention problems. Table 16 specifically addresses positive behavior strategies that can be employed by a classroom teacher for dealing with attention problems or behaviors in students associated with ADHD.

Functional Behavioral Assessment

On occasion, there will be a student who does not respond to the positive behavior supports you are implementing in your classroom, so you will have to consider using a program that is more individualized. This is going to require some level of assessment to develop an effective program. A functional behavioral assessment (FBA) is a problem-solving process for addressing problem behaviors. It is usually reserved for more serious, recurring problems that do not respond to classroom management techniques. The FBA involves a variety of techniques and strategies to identify the purposes of a specific behavior and to develop interventions to remediate the problem behavior.

• •

Functional behavioral assessment (FBA): A problem-solving process for addressing students' behaviors.

• •

The rationale for conducting an FBA is that nearly all behaviors occur within a particular context and serve a specific focus. Students learn to behave in ways that result in a desired outcome. For example, if Student A seems to start fights with other classmates every day during math class, and he consistently gets

Table 16
Strategies for Managing the Behaviors of Students With ADHD

For the Classroom Teacher

- Be prepared to refocus or recue students frequently.
- Be prepared to repeat rules and instructions.
- Repeat explanations of consequences for both positive and negative behavior choices.
- Use immediate consequences (praise, rewards, privileges) for task completion as appropriate.
- Employ activities and consequences of high interest to the student.
- Start incentives before punishments in the management program.
- Strive for consistency in expectations for the child and all significant adults' responses to him.
- Anticipate problem situations and activities.
- Develop realistic expectations for what he can and cannot be held accountable for in developing goals for his behavior.
- Practice forgiveness.
- Coordinate all management techniques in school with parents in an integrated fashion, so that the same rules apply and receive follow-up in all situations.
- It is suggested that a contract system might be employed to be sure that the child is keeping track of his assignments. Parents should sign off daily on a contract outlining appropriate consequences and special privileges for degrees of completion.
- Select one person at school to coordinate communications between school and the parents in order to maintain consistency.
- The child may benefit from external cues or calming techniques to focus on the whole message being delivered and for the relevant cues to be considered. A consistent gesture or signal for all of the child's teachers to use in regaining her attention should be developed and practiced.
- Highly structured routines and specific instructions should be implemented.
- Peripheral stimulation can be distracting. The child could be seated in such a way that distracting influences are minimized. He should not be placed in the back of the room or next to the window where he will constantly be subjected to distracting influences. Usually, a seat near the front of the room close to the teacher will help him maintain attention.
- Be sure to keep unnecessary materials off of the student's desk. Extraneous materials should be put away immediately after use.
- Explicit directions for each step of the learning process must be indicated clearly. Short tasks with a clear end in sight and a reinforcement for each step of the learning process are effective ways of helping students complete lengthy assignments.
- Utilize time-out if necessary.
- Allow the child to have passes to permit interruptions. Reward unused interruption passes.
- Use a visual focal point on the blackboard or the teacher's hand, to form a habitual place for the child to refocus.

- Use a brief relaxation, meditation, or quiet calming activity to allow the student to recenter himself.
- It is also sometimes effective to permit a "squeeze ball" or other unobtrusive and safe manipulative to keep hands busy when they are temporarily idle.
- Identify one or more areas of strength, talent, and interest to build self-esteem and confidence.
- Don't leave your class unattended.
- Prioritize multiple tasks.
- Develop a timeline for long-term projects.
- Utilize study guides, outlines, and charts for following progress.
- Ensure in class that homework assignments have been noted and understood before leaving for the day.
- Break down large tasks into smaller clear chunks, which can be reviewed and monitored sequentially.
- For nonroutine tasks, develop a simple calendar and "to do" list. For routine tasks, utilize a daily responsibilities list with clear consequences for compliance/noncompliance.
- Keep an envelope for important papers attached to his school notebook to be checked regularly by his parents.

For Parents

- A physician who is able to consider possible pharmacological interventions and monitor the medicine's effectiveness should see the child regularly.
- A program of home and school management should be employed including the use of contracts, natural consequences for behavior, and other techniques.
- The student can frequently gain improvement from counseling to help him explore his feelings and reactions to his attention needs, to explore their implications and the adjustments to be expected with medications or other interventions, and to act as an advocate for himself in requiring appropriate accommodations.
- Therapeutic consultation for the child's parents is suggested so that they may be able to work together in developing and sustaining a shared, effective management plan.
- The child can gain from social skills groups and/or summer camps available for students with similar needs.
- Use a phone network of classmates to check on assignments as necessary.

From *School Success for Kids With Asperger's Syndrome* by S. M. Silverman and R. Weinfeld, 2007, pp. 216–218, Waco, TX: Prufrock Press. Copyright 2007 Prufrock Press. Reprinted with permission.

removed from the classroom, maybe he has learned an effective way to avoid academic demands that are beyond his capabilities. Therefore, identifying the purpose of the problem behavior—or more specifically, what the student gains, controls, or avoids—can provide useful information in assisting the teacher in developing instructional and behavioral strategies that can reduce inappropriate behaviors.

Conducting an FBA

According to IDEA (2004), if a student with a disability is exhibiting behavior problems, his or her needs must be addressed in the IEP. Any teachers that the student may have should be involved in developing the IEP because they will be responsible for implementing it. When behavior has to be addressed, the IEP team must include a behavioral intervention plan (BIP) based on information from the FBA.

There may be a school-based group that handles prereferrals for special education and could assist in conducting the FBA, but it is not unusual for the special education teacher to be in charge of implementation. As a special education teacher, this is something you should know how to do. Below is a summary of the steps involved in conducting an FBA.

1. Identify and define the problem behavior.
2. Collect data to determine the function of the behavior.
3. Form a hypothesis about the function of the behavior.
4. Develop and implement the intervention plan.
5. Collect data to determine success.

Different behaviors may require different data collection methods. One of the most basic techniques consists of direct observation. This involves observing the problem behavior and describing the conditions that surround the behavior (context). The context includes antecedents, which are the events or activities preceding the problem behavior, and the consequences, which follow the problem behavior. There are several data sheets that can be used to collect this information, but two of the most frequently used by classroom teachers are a scatter plot and an ABC chart.

The scatter plot is an interval recording method that can be used to identify patterns of behavior that are associated with the contextual conditions. The scatter plot is a grid divided into periods of time. For instance, the time listed on the grid might be divided into 15-minute periods. You may want shorter or longer time periods depending on the type of behavior and length of time for the observation. The scatter plot provides a graphic display of the relationship between two variables. It is useful in the early stages of analysis when exploring data on a student. On a scatter plot, an observer records single events (e.g., number of student call-outs) or a series of events (e.g., teacher requests and student responses) that occur within a given context (e.g., during teacher-led reading instruction, at lunch, on the playground). Information obtained from a scatter plot can then show the teacher if there is a relationship between the behaviors and help the teacher to formulate ideas to either reduce the undesired behavior or increase the desired behavior. For example, if data shows that a student has a large number of call-outs at the very beginning of class and that is causing a problem with instruction, then the teacher could investigate specifically what is happening at the beginning of class to cause this student behavior and what the teacher can do to try to reduce this behavior. See Appendix C for a completed scatter plot and Appendix D for a blank scatter plot.

One of the most common data collection methods used is the Antecedent-Behavior-Consequence (ABC) chart, which is used to record descriptive information while observing a student. This approach allows the observer to organize the descriptive information in order to look for patterns of behavior within the conditions surrounding the behavior. See Appendix E for a completed ABC chart and Appendix F for a blank ABC chart.

• •

Antecedent-Behavior-Consequence chart: A form used to log instances of observed behavior in order to systematically identify the variables that may precede/trigger or follow/maintain target behavior.

• •

Realistically, you will not always be able to observe all of the events that bring about or maintain the problem behavior, so interviews will also be used to gather data. Use of interviews with teachers, parents, school staff members, and other adults who have direct contact with the student will provide additional information regarding the contextual factors of the behavior.

Once an FBA has been conducted, you will need to examine all of the data that has been collected and form a hypothesis about why the behavior is occurring or what is the function of the behavior. For example, is the student exhibiting the behavior to seek something she wants or is the student exhibiting the behavior to escape or avoid a task or something undesired? Consider that the student may be trying to get attention from you or her peers, but she may also be trying to avoid a difficult academic task. At that point, you have to consider whether or not she has a skills deficit.

If a student is being asked to perform a behavioral or academic skill that she does not know how to perform or that may be very difficult for her to perform, the student may prefer to engage in inappropriate behavior so the task can be avoided. For example, a student may prefer to kick a classmate and be removed from class instead of admit that she struggles with a particular academic skill. School is very peer driven, and some students prefer to act out inappropriately instead of risking the chance that their peers may make fun of them for struggling academically. This happens more often than you would think.

Although these are effective tools to assist you in performing an FBA, this can be a lengthy and challenging process. Determining the function of behaviors takes time, consistency, and patience.

Behavior Intervention Plan (BIP)

Once the FBA is completed, the special education teacher, school psychologist, or behavior specialist will develop a BIP that will use the information gathered to create a concrete plan of action for addressing a student's behavior. A BIP may include ways to change the environment to keep behavior from starting in the first place, provide positive reinforcement to promote good behavior, employ planned ignoring to avoid reinforcing bad behavior, and provide supports needed so that the student will not be driven to act out due to frustration or fatigue. When a behavior plan is agreed upon, the school and staff are legally obligated to follow it, and consequences of not following it should not be inflicted on the student. In other words, this is not just left up to you as the special education teacher. The components of a BIP include:

- target behaviors;
- specific, measurable goals;
- intervention description and method;
- start date and frequency of intervention;
- method of evaluation;
- persons responsible for each part of the intervention and evaluation; and
- data from the evaluation.

Once the BIP is completed, the IEP team will meet to approve the plan and the implementation can begin. It will also be important to set a time to meet briefly with all individuals responsible for implementing the plan to evaluate progress. See Appendix G for a blank BIP plan.

Managing With Success

Effective teaching requires much more than just knowing the content areas. Without reasonable control over your classroom, you will have minimal success with your students. As a new or experienced special education teacher, you will quickly find that classroom management skills are necessary to run a smooth classroom. By establishing and consistently applying clear classroom rules, procedures, and routines, teachers can prevent the likelihood of many students' inappropriate behaviors from initially occurring. Your ability to effectively use behavior supports will produce a positive learning environment for all students and allow you the much-needed time to focus on teaching. It is easy to become overwhelmed with a new job, new responsibilities, and new students, so seek out experienced teachers and related personnel in your building or district who can help you develop and implement the system that is best for your classroom.

◇◇◇

SURVIVAL SECRETS OF TEACHERS

Alicia, Elementary Special Education Teacher

What Is Your Current Position and How Long Have You Been Teaching?

I am currently teaching third-, fourth-, and fifth-grade special education in both inclusion and self-contained classrooms. I have been teaching for 5 years.

What Were Some of the Issues With Classroom Management You Faced as a First-Year Teacher?

My first experience in a classroom was in a middle school in the Bronx, New York City. I was a NYC Teaching Fellow and was essentially "thrown to the wolves" as far as teaching was concerned. My special education classroom was made up of 12 students, one instructional aide, and one teacher. The students had emotional disabilities, learning disabilities, or intellectual disabilities. It was a sixth-grade class, and I remember walking in with my pencil skirt and heels on, all the way up to the fourth floor of an un-air-conditioned building and realizing very quickly this was going to be quite different from the sales work I was used to.

Although most of our university summer prep courses taught [us] that we (teachers) should have a method or strategy to use for dealing with behavior management, there were few examples offered. Some did the marble jar (does that really work?); others discussed ways to "control" your class by giving stickers or some type of incentive. Luckily, the teachers at my new school worked in teams, and I quickly became aware of how important consistency was going to be with whatever behavior program I chose to use.

What Type of Behavior Plan Did You Use?

The program that I ended up using consisted of behavior plan folders, and I used it as a classwide system. Each folder included one sheet for each day of the week. For each class the students went to, they received a "grade" of 1, 2, 3, 4, or 5 depending on how well they behaved. We had specific behavioral criteria for each number. The classes for the students were listed daily and at the end of the day/week the scores were added up. Depending on the number of classes, the students were also given rewards for their behavior if their scores were above a certain number. This plan also helped motivate the class as a group rather than just individuals. Because communication with parents is so important, this gave us data and documentation that we could show parents. It was also helpful to be able to look back and see how the students were progressing. The folder was a great tool in middle school because a student was assigned to carry it with him, and it went from teacher to teacher. This was essential in middle school when the class traveled together, but had different teachers for all of their subjects.

What Changes Have You Made in Terms of Behavior Management Since You First Began Teaching?

What I learned very quickly in my first teaching job was that the more prepared I was as a teacher, the more respect and attention I had from the students. I found that if the daily schedule was written on the board and an AIM (question about what we were doing that day; e.g., what is figurative language and how do we use it in our writing?) was presented and clearly stated, then the students knew my expectations for the period and were more likely to get settled and start listening. If I was unprepared (e.g., finishing copies, at my desk, talking to another teacher), then the class was not ready to get started. I felt like if I "winged" it a lot trying to come up with something, then I was unclear about how it would work, and thus my rambling wouldn't keep their attention. If it didn't seem like I knew what I was talking about, then they took advantage of that and the behaviors and disruptions were continuous.

Currently, I implement individual behavior systems for my students. Each student earns a ticket for exhibiting appropriate behavior. Students know my behavioral expectations, and I try to be consistent. Some students need a daily behavior management sheet where they earn tickets immediately throughout the day. I can be more flexible with some of the other students, and they can wait until the end of the day to collect their tickets. At the end of the week, they can turn in their tickets and choose a prize. Regardless of how simple I think the prizes are, they always seem to work! I currently have 20 students on my caseload and each one has a folder on my desk where I put their tickets. If I forget, you can rest assured they will ask me if they earned a ticket. It has really been a great tool in my class.

◇◇◇

Conclusion

To teach in an inclusive classroom, the teacher must effectively manage student behavior. Students will be unable to learn and progress through the curriculum if there is not a conducive learning environment. Teachers must be able to manage behavior in their classroom, while at the same time motivate their students to learn to their fullest potential. To help do this, teachers must be proactive and set the tone for the classroom learning environment by establishing classroom rules and procedures, incorporating classwide positive behavior supports, and implementing functional behavioral assessment. In addition, teachers in inclusive classrooms must realize that behavior is impacted by the classroom, the students, the situation, and sometimes the teacher, so determining what will be the best plan of action will be different for each situation.

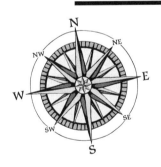

Survival Tips

- Plan some time at the beginning of the year for team building or group activities so that students can experience community in the classroom.

- Set aside one-on-one time with your students before, during, or after class to give feedback and praise for successful self-monitoring behavior.

- Never assume problem behaviors occur across settings; where and when problem behaviors occur can be valuable information in identifying triggers for behavior.

Survival Toolkit

Websites to Support You With Classroom Management

- Classroom Management for Teachers.com: http://www.classroommanagementforteachers.com
- Classroom Management Strategies That Work: http://www.theteachersguide.com/ClassManagement.htm
- Classroom Management Tips for Teachers!: http://www.teachingheart.net/classroommanagementtips.html
- Classroom Management: http://www.proteacher.com/030000.shtml

Books to Help You With Classroom Management\

MacKenzie, R. J., & Stanzione, L. E. (2010). *Setting limits in the classroom: A complete guide to effective classroom management with a school-wide discipline plan* (3rd ed.). New York, NY: Three Rivers Press.

Simon Weinstein, C., Romano, M. E., & Mignano, A. J., Jr. (2010). *Elementary classroom management: Lessons from research and practice* (5th ed.). New York, NY: McGraw-Hill.

Springer, S., Alexander, B., & Persiani-Becker, K. (2005). *The organized teacher: A hands-on guide to setting up and running a terrific classroom.* New York, NY: McGraw-Hill.

Tincani, M. (2011). *Preventing challenging behavior in your classroom: Positive behavior support and effective classroom management.* Waco, TX: Prufrock Press.

8 Using Data to Support IEP Goals

Assessment is an important piece of the puzzle for teachers in an inclusive classroom. What type of assessment do you use? Which assessment is most appropriate for the behavior to be assessed? These questions and more were discussed in Chapter Six on assessment. This chapter expands that information to address the results of the assessment. What did you find out? Where is the student functioning? How does this relate to and support IEP goals? This chapter will focus on interpreting results and discussing how assessment and instruction fit together.

Informal and formal data about student learning not only shape instruction but also determine its effectiveness. It is important to implement multiple methods of data collection and view the process as dynamic and continuous. The role of a data collector is three dimensional: (a) to determine students' prior understanding and achievement, (b) to track their responses to moderate challenges, and (c) to measure their outcomes against expected performance goals (Brimijoin, 2002; Tomlinson, 1995).

Assessment is a powerful tool that needs to be integrated throughout the entire process of teaching and learning, and it demands the same kind of evaluation skills that good teachers use for effective classroom management (Brimijoin, Marquissee, & Tomlinson, 2003). Using measures of student learning that are not sensitive to the actual learning occurring in classrooms is the first mistake. This commonly happens when a school or district relies on what is referred to as "indirect" learning data, often provided by off-the-shelf standardized tests and even state-level standardized tests. Such measures are indirect because they frequently do not adequately assess the content that is actually taught in a given school. A school might, in fact, be producing impressive student learning gains, but the test data do not pick that up (Marzano, 2003). However, the most important reason for the collection of educational data on children is to ensure and improve the quality of outcomes.

Teachers can graph students' performance over time to determine whether students are making progress toward achieving their instructional goals. When students' performance slopes are relatively flat, teachers can modify instruction to target deficits and then evaluate instructional outcomes. See Figure 15 for an example of a curriculum-based measurement (CBM) graph. In this example, the intervention is effective at improving the students' performance over time.

Collecting data is only the beginning. The data have to be graphed to show a visual representation. A list of students' scores can go unchallenged, but if data are graphed and visually inspected on a continual basis, then student growth or lack of it can be seen (formative assessment), as well as students' overall performance (summative assessment). It is important to point out that a curriculum-based measurement graph, with its multiple references, creates opportunities for clearer communication. It has now become common practice for teachers to use the CBM data in parent conferences and at multidisciplinary team meetings to provide a framework for communicating individual students' statuses. Professional educators and parents can easily use the CBM graph because little or no interpretation of the scores is necessary (Shinn, Habedank, & Good, 1993). Not only does the collection of student data indicate how a particular student or group of students is doing, but it also tells the teacher how he or she is doing and the effectiveness of the intervention.

The Impact of Making Decisions Without Using Data

When decisions regarding student performance and intervention implementation are not driven by data, it can turn out to be a hit or miss scenario. How does the teacher know how a student is actually performing? How do teachers know if they are doing a good job? How do they know if the interventions chosen are effective? All of these questions arise when data is not collected. If an intervention is chosen that has no data support, then teachers will be taking a chance on whether it is effective or not. Granted, not all interventions that have data support will necessarily work with all students; however, there is a better chance than not that they will be effective.

Data also help teachers in their decision-making abilities regarding student, teacher, and intervention performance. Data form a rationale or guidelines for

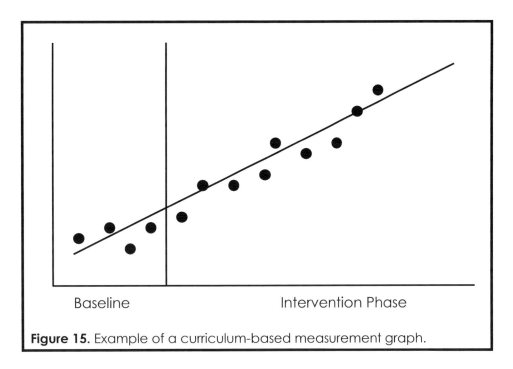

Baseline   Intervention Phase

Figure 15. Example of a curriculum-based measurement graph.

decision making. Without the collection of data, the proper decisions may not be made and teaching time could be sacrificed.

Outcomes of Using Data in Decision Making

When data are incorporated into the decision-making process, communication among other teachers, school personnel, and parents will be formulated. If teachers can show others that what they are doing in their classroom is effective, or that they are making changes based on data, then others involved with the child or children will more easily understand the teacher's decision. The collection of data on a continuous, consistent basis will help with knowing and communicating about student performance.

Madaus, Kellaghan, Rakow, and King (1979) noticed that when schools used indirect tests to measure student achievement, the schools did not appear to be very effective, but when they used direct tests—those that actually measured the content that teachers taught in the school—some schools looked highly effective (cited in Marzano, 2003). The National Research Council (2003) concluded that standardized tests and state tests based on standards certainly have their place in the landscape of K–12 education, but schools should not use them as the primary indicator of student learning. A school must use assessments that actually measure the content that teachers teach (Marzano, 2003), which means schools should use something in addition to standardized tests.

Data-Based Decision Making–The Process

The use of data in making decisions requires (a) deliberate collection (identifying critical data to have and measure); (b) analysis (with frequency that allows responsive changes in programs or interventions); (c) data-driven decisions (decisions that are made only after questions are answered with data to back up problem identification and intervention selection); and (d) data-based evaluation and accountability. Data help to frame our questions about student performance, design and implement interventions, and ask the critical question throughout the process—"Is there a better way?" Therefore, accountability is a process that includes measurement, data collection, decision making, and evaluation (Isaacs, 2003).

Other questions include (McTighe & Thomas, 2003):

- What strengths and weaknesses in student performance do the different data sources reveal?
- Are these the results that were expected? Why or why not?
- In what areas did the students perform best? What weaknesses are evident?
- How are different population groups performing on the various assessments? What does this work reveal about student learning and performance?
- What patterns or changes can be observed over time? Are there any surprises? What results are unexpected? What anomalies exist?
- Is there evidence of improvement or decline? If so, what might have caused the changes?
- What questions do these data raise? Are these results consistent with other achievement data? Are there alternative explanations for these results?
- By what criteria are we evaluating student work?

When data are collected, it is essential that they are analyzed in detail to see what they really tell us about the student(s), the teacher, and the instructional practices.

Identifying the Problem

How do teachers know what is the problem? Observation could be one way the problem is identified, by observing the student in comparison to his peers, as well as where he should be developmentally. Another example is work samples. Collecting student work samples and comparing the performance to others, as well as where the student should be developmentally, could also identify the problem. Finally, parents or others involved with the child might raise a concern to the teacher and then observations, work samples, or both could be implemented to see if there is a problem and to document what the actual problem is. Specifically identifying the problem is crucial in order to start the process of remediation.

Setting the Goal

Although writing measurable goals is a critical first step in deciding the nature and scope of services for a student, it is not sufficient to ensure educational benefit to students. A method for measuring progress toward goals must be developed. Progress monitoring consists of five steps (Hagan-Burke & Jefferson, 2002):

1. establish an annual goal,
2. set the expected rate of progress,
3. measure progress toward that goal at least weekly,
4. compare a student's actual progress with the student's expected progress, and
5. make appropriate instructional decisions.

Goal setting and progress monitoring do not need to be time-consuming tasks and may easily be accomplished using curriculum-based assessment (CBA) and CBM. CBA and CBM measures are sensitive to subtle progress and may be administered at least weekly. CBA includes any measures derived from the student's general education curriculum typically developed by the teacher, whereas CBM measures are derived from the student's annual curriculum and may be purchased from an existing CBM library or developed according to standard procedures (Shinn, 1997). First, individual student performance during an initial baseline phase is collected, and those data are plotted on a graph. Second, a goal line is established. A goal line connecting the initial level and the goal depicts the rate of improvement necessary for the student to achieve the goal. Third, for every five data points a vertical line is drawn on the graph. The vertical lines on the graph indicate the point at which a decision is made regarding a possible change in the student's program. At each point, judgments are made regarding the effectiveness of the instruction being provided. This systematic approach to setting goals, monitoring growth, changing programs, and evaluating the effects of changes is the formative evaluation model. Research on the achievement effects of using this approach has revealed that the students of teachers who use systematic formative evaluation based on CBM have greater achievement rates (Fuchs, Deno, & Mirkin, 1984) than those whose teachers choose not to implement it. See Figures 16–18 for examples of the baseline, goal line, and progress monitoring graphs.

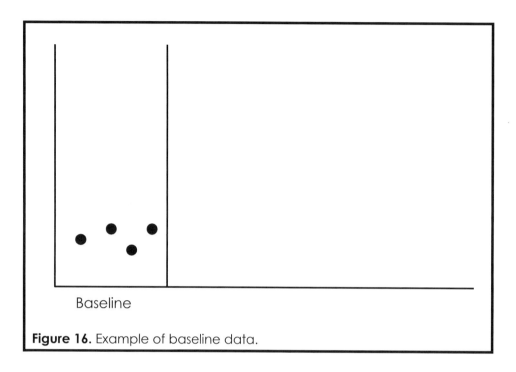

Baseline

Figure 16. Example of baseline data.

In Figure 16, the teacher has collected baseline data and plotted them on the graph. These data are collected prior to implementation of any intervention to establish the student's current level of performance. It is important to help the teacher document if an intervention is effective or not.

In Figure 17, the teacher has collected baseline data and plotted them on the graph. In addition, the teacher has drawn a goal level line. Based on the baseline data, the teacher draws this line to indicate intended progress over time. This line is important when collecting intervention data. The goal line will help the teacher determine if the intervention is effective or not and if any changes need to be made.

In Figure 18, baseline data were collected and then plotted on the graph. The teacher then plotted a goal line. The goal line is a standard that the teacher can use to compare progress data over time. As noted, after the teacher collected five data points (after baseline) the data indicated that the student was *not* making progress toward the goal and the intervention was either modified or changed. Based upon this change, the data indicated that the new intervention was effective and the student was on track toward reaching her desired goal.

Deciding What Data to Collect

Gunter (2001) defined data collection in school settings as the systematic gathering of information designed to verify that student learning occurs. Many types of data are gathered for this purpose, including grades, work samples, and

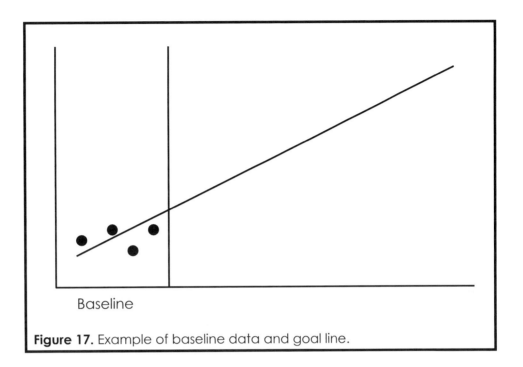

Figure 17. Example of baseline data and goal line.

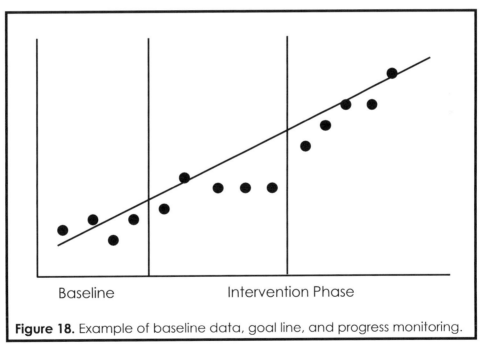

Figure 18. Example of baseline data, goal line, and progress monitoring.

anecdotal notes (Gunter, Callicott, Denny, & Gerber, 2003). Data collection is the foundation of informed teacher decision making and is the basis for the IEP (Gunter et al., 2003). It is important that the correct data are collected so that the problem the student is having is supported.

Once the behavior is specifically identified and an operational definition of the behavior is formulated, the selection of the correct data collection technique can happen. It is important to choose the correct method of data collection for the behavior; otherwise, the actual behavior, as well as progress and teacher and intervention effectiveness, could be sacrificed. Choosing the wrong data collection method could have some serious consequences. If the incorrect method is chosen, then the teacher may not accurately record the behavior he is trying to observe. It is important to choose the correct method to match the anticipated behavior.

Data Collection Methods and Their Purposes

Tawney and Gast (1984) described formative evaluation as an ongoing process with frequent (at least weekly) and repeated measurement of students' performance. They indicated that such evaluation can be used to guide instruction and confirm achievement of objectives. Formative assessment is critical in telling the teacher how he is doing as well as how the students are doing. Without formative assessment, teachers' perceptions of students' performance compared to students' actual performance are often erroneous (Fuchs et al., 1984). In addition, teachers trained in formative assessment procedures may be more open to changing instructional methods and making more frequent instructional changes to promote achievement (Bloom, Hursh, Wienke, & Wold, 1992; Fuchs et al., 1984).

Fuchs and Fuchs (1986) presented three aspects of formative evaluation procedures that directly relate to the achievement of students with disabilities. First, effect sizes—the statistical description of the educational impact—were significantly increased when behavior modification procedures such as incorporating reinforcement were paired with systematic measurement. Second, when data evaluation rules were used to make decisions regarding when educational programs should be changed, increases in effect sizes were significant. Finally, when data were graphed rather than simply recorded, there were significant increases noted in student outcomes.

When observing behaviors, teachers participate in anecdotal recording, event recording, latency recording, duration recording, interval recording, and time sampling. Anecdotal recording is writing down everything that happens regarding a specific student in a particular environment or setting. This might be used if a teacher is really not sure what behaviors are problems and may help the teacher to better focus on what is actually happening. Oftentimes the collection of these data will lead to more data collection using one of the methods below to precisely identify what is happening. For all of the data collection methods, it is important to note that the person observing the student and behavior should make his observations based on a specific behavioral definition. For example, on-task behavior could be defined as when the student is doing what the teacher has instructed the student to do (e.g., independent practice activities, listening to a lecture, taking notes).

Event recording is collecting the frequency (number of times) of a behavior for a given time or period. Typically, the observer would just tally the number of times the behavior was observed (e.g., "The student got out of his seat four times during the 30-minute science lesson"). Latency recording collects the amount of time it takes a student to start an activity or exhibit a particular behavior. Typically, the observer would record the amount of time it took the student to exhibit the behavior starting with the teacher prompt. For example, "It took the student 2 minutes and 45 seconds to start her homework assignment once instructed to do so." Duration recording is collecting the amount of time a behavior lasts. Typically, the observer would record the amount of time the student exhibited the behavior during a given time or period. For example, "The student had a temper tantrum that lasted 3 minutes and 22 seconds."

Those who want to find the proportion of a specified time period during which the behavior occurs may select interval recording or time sampling. Both of these data collection methods record an approximation of the actual number of times a behavior occurs. For interval recording, a set time of the interval is chosen (say every 30 seconds) and if the behavior occurs at any time in the interval it is marked. For time sampling, a set time is also chosen (say 1 minute) and if the behavior occurs at the end of the interval it is marked. See Table 17 for a description and comparison of different data collection methods and associated purposes. See Appendices H–K for some sample data collection forms.

Establishing Baseline

Establishing a baseline simply means measuring a student's skills prior to intervention (e.g., instruction). Once established, this baseline becomes the yardstick against which a teacher can measure the effectiveness of any intervention (Hagan-Burke & Jefferson, 2002). For example, establishing a baseline for Miguel can be accomplished by having him read aloud for 1 minute from each of three second-grade CBM reading passages. The teacher notes how many words Miguel read correctly in each 1-minute sample and tracks how many errors he made. These three 1-minute samples of reading behavior provide a starting point for goal setting and measuring progress.

Table 17
Data Collection Methods and Associated Purposes

Data collection method	Use
Anecdotal recording	A brief narrative description of an event or events that the observer felt was important to observe.
Permanent product recording	Analyzing student products or work that has been completed, focusing on the process (what the student did to get the answer) as well as the product (the correct answer).
Running record (continuous record)	A description of events as they occur. Everything that the student does is written down.
Event recording	The number of times something happens or that a behavior occurs.
Duration recording	A measure of the length of time a specific event or behavior lasts.
Intensity recording	A measure of the degree of a behavior expressed as high, medium, or low.
Latency recording	The amount of time between a request to begin a behavior or event and when the student begins the requested behavior or event.
Interval recording	An observational method that involves recording specific events or behaviors (that occur frequently) during a prespecified time interval (e.g., 1 minute).
Time sampling	An observational method that involves recording specific events or behaviors at the end of a prespecified time interval (e.g., 1 minute).
Error analysis	This goes beyond marking answers as correct or incorrect and analyzes the mistakes to see if there is an error pattern for the student. This might help the teacher to focus his instruction differently.

The next step is to plot this information on a graph and decide how much progress Miguel is expected to make within a 20-week time period. To determine an expected rate of progress for Miguel, the teacher considers his baseline rate of 20 words read correctly per minute for each of the three reading passages. Next the teacher decides how much progress Miguel should make in 20 weeks given effective instruction. As a starting point, it might be anticipated that Miguel will gain 2 correct words per week—a gain of 40 words in 20 weeks (2 words per week x 20 weeks; Hagan-Burke & Jefferson, 2002).

Deciding When to Collect Data

When and how often should a teacher collect data? That is really up to the teacher, but the more often a teacher collects data and on a consistent basis, the better off the student(s) and teacher. The decision of how often the teacher collects data can have serious implications for intervention implementation as well as student and teacher progress and effectiveness of teaching time. For example, assume that a teacher collects three to five intervention data samples prior to making a decision on whether the student(s) are performing up to goals previously set and whether the teacher and intervention are being effective. If the teacher collects formal data once a week, then a decision would be able to be made after 3–5 weeks depending on the data that were collected. If the same teacher only collected formal data once a month, then a decision by that same teacher would be only be able to be made after 3–5 months. In the first scenario, a change could be made after 3–5 weeks, whereas in the second scenario a change would not be made until 3–5 months had passed. That difference is a total of 7–15 weeks that the teacher is actually implementing something with the child that may not be effective. If the student is doing well and the intervention is effective, then it might not make a difference; however, if the student is not doing well and the intervention is not effective, then a lot of time is being wasted on something that is not working.

Communicating Assessment Results to Parents and Teachers

Given that most teachers and parents will not have knowledge or expertise in the area of assessment, a critical component of getting these individuals involved with the assessment process is to effectively communicate the assessment results to them. What do the results mean? How does the child compare to other students? What is the course of action to remediate the difficulties the child is having? It is the role of the teacher to effectively communicate the assessment results to parents and other teachers. One of the best ways is to show the results visually. In addition to using quantitative results (numbers), actually graphing those numbers and showing participants the results is highly recommended. Just spouting off numbers can be very intimidating to those in attendance at a meeting and can cause participants to shut down for fear of being depicted as lacking the expertise to be involved. On the other hand, if you were to communicate the numbers, but also incorporate a graph or visual representation of the results, then it would be easier for those in attendance to understand and then they might be more apt to participate in the discussion. Making the data accessible and understandable to teachers and parents is key to getting them involved in this part of the assessment process.

SURVIVAL SECRETS OF TEACHERS

Heidi, High School Special Education Teacher

What Is Your Current Position and How Long Have You Been Teaching?

In my current position I am a high school teacher who works in inclusion and resource classrooms. I have been teaching for 6 years.

What Were Some of the Issues You Faced With Using Data as a First-Year Teacher?

I think the biggest issue was getting organized with all of the students I was working with. Each student had a different set of goals and objectives in a multitude of different areas and at first it was very difficult for me to figure out what data I needed to collect for each student and how I was going to do that. To solve this, I needed to take some time with each student's IEP and figure out what I was going to do and how I was going to do it. I also had an issue on how I was going to collect and store the data. Would I use a folder, the computer, or a spreadsheet? It seemed to vary for each student and each situation. For most students I used a spreadsheet. This gave me the latitude to either present the numbers or plot them into some type of chart or graph. In other cases, I kept notes or other kinds of data. The big thing was to not just do the same thing for each student. Just like each IEP was individualized, I needed to learn that each data plan had to be individualized as well.

How Did Other Teachers Use Data?

When I came to my school, other teachers in the building did not use data effectively. They collected homework and assigned scores or grades, and then they used exams for end-of-the-unit assessments. They never made the connection between assessment and instruction and how the two were linked. They often followed the curriculum and felt each day had to be a new topic and new assignment to be able to make it through the curriculum by the end of the year. In working with other teachers I was able to communicate to them that homework has more than one function. In addition to telling the teacher if the student understands the concept, it can also tell the teacher if she has done a good job teaching the content and, in some cases, if she needs to reteach the content before she moves on. For example, if more than half the class does poorly on an assignment, then it could mean that they didn't understand what was taught, the teacher did not do a good job teaching the content, or both. As a teacher, you wouldn't want to move forward and build upon something students didn't understand. If this kept happening, then students would just fall farther and farther behind. It is important to analyze all data regarding student performance.

What Advice Would You Give Future Teachers About Using Data?

Data are the key to student performance. In an age of RtI and evidence-based practices, it is important to collect data. You can collect data on behavior or academics. First, find out the student's current functioning level. Now you can implement a strategy. Continue to collect data consistently and frequently. Data will tell you how a student is doing, how you are doing as a teacher, and how the strategy implemented is doing. Data can also help you to communicate with others including other teachers, parents, and administrators. You can look at progress over time as well as compare the effectiveness of different instructional procedures. There are opportunities to collect data every day, but you just need to know what to collect and when to collect the information. Data do not have to be from an exam, but can be from an observation, homework, or a multitude of other sources. Learn to use data effectively and you will have a much better grasp on your students' progress as well as your own teaching.

◇◇◇

Conclusion

Data collection is just one piece of the puzzle when teachers are working with students in an inclusive classroom. It is very important to find out where students are performing in the different academic areas and to assess how students are performing behaviorally in the classroom. Data collection will also aide the teacher when developing IEPs and evaluating goals and objectives. At the very beginning of the teaching process, it is important to find out the students' current functioning levels. After the data are collected, the teacher must interpret the results and develop a plan of action based on the results. From there, teachers can work with a team to develop an IEP to guide each student, teacher, and parent to make sure adequate progress is being made. The critical factor is that data collection needs to be implemented frequently and consistently to monitor the progress of both students and teachers. By doing so, teachers will find success and be able to make modifications to their teaching to benefit their students and themselves.

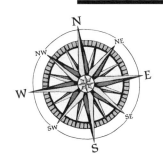

Survival Tips

- Teachers often do not realize that they already possess a lot of data in students' permanent products such as homework, quizzes, and written assignments.

- Develop a system for collecting student data. This will help you keep your records updated and ensure that you are implementing the IEP goals.

- Your colleagues should be able to provide examples of data collection forms and how they can be used to represent progress on the IEP goals.

Survival Toolkit

Websites to Support You With Data and IEP Goals

- Linking Teacher and Student Data to Improve Teacher and Teaching Quality: http://www.dataqualitycampaign.org/files/Meetings-DQC_Quarterly_Issue_Brief_031207.pdf

- Using Classroom Data to Improve Student Achievement: http://www.classroomdata.org

- Data Collection Strategies: http://www.circleofinclusion.org/english/pim/seven/strategies.html

- Teachers' Use of Data to Impact Teaching and Learning: http://www.all4ed.org/events/081309TeachersUseOfData

- Analyzing Classroom Assessment Data: http://www.classroomdata.org/index.cfm?page=3

- Measurable IEP Goals: http://www.concordspedpac.org/IEPGoals.html

- IEPs & 504 Plans–Sample Plans, Goals and Objectives: http://www.familyvillage.wisc.edu/education/iepsamples.html

Books to Support You With IEP Development

Bateman, B. D., & Herr, C. M. (2003). *Writing measurable IEP goals and objectives*. Verona, WI: Attainment Company.

Bateman, B. D. (2007). *From gobbledygook to clearly written annual IEP goals*. Verona, WI: Attainment Company.

Eason, A. I., & Whitbread, K. (2006). *IEP and inclusion tips for parents and teachers*. Verona, WI: Attainment Company.

Herr, C. M., & Bateman, B. D. (2006). *Better IEP meetings: Everyone wins.* Verona, WI: Attainment Company.

Pierangelo, R., & Giuliani, G. A. (2007). *Understanding, developing, and writing effective IEPs: A step-by-step guide for educators*. Thousand Oaks, CA: Corwin Press.

Schwarz, S. P., & McKinney, N. K. (2005). *Organizing your IEPs*. Verona, WI: Attainment Company.

Wright, P. W. D., Wright, P. D., & O'Connor, S. W. (2010). *Wrightslaw: All about IEPs: Answers to frequently asked questions about IEPs*. Hartfield, VA: Harbor House Law Press.

9 Technology

When you are hired as a teacher to teach in an inclusive classroom, one area that will be instrumental for your success is technology. Every day, more and more technology is developed, and as an inclusion teacher it will be very important that you are aware of the technology available that could benefit you and your students, particularly assistive technologies developed to aid students with disabilities. Being aware is one thing, but you must also be able to operate the technology and be able to implement it within the curriculum. Many school districts provide professional development opportunities to train teachers in the use of technology. Things to consider include: (a) access/opportunities of technology and assistive technology, (b) knowledge of operating systems, (c) technology training, and (d) technology support.

Technology has changed the lives of many people and that includes teachers. Our educational system relies heavily on technology. Students are using smart phones, laptops, and netbooks, and teachers are implementing smart boards, electronic gradebooks, and blogs about their daily teaching routine. Communication now occurs through e-mail or some type of social network (e.g., Twitter, Facebook). The world is constantly changing around us and so must our instruction, when appropriate. Technology can make a learning experience more meaningful, and teachers must be able to decide when to effectively implement technology in their instruction. Obviously, a teacher in an inclusive classroom should not be expected to know everything about technology, but she should have some knowledge or at least know where to acquire information available about technology options.

Assistive Technology

Technology can be very important to the inclusive classroom teacher in order to meet all students' needs. One option is to incorporate assistive technology. Assistive technology (AT) is defined by the Technology-Related Assistance for Individuals with Disabilities Act of 1988 (Tech Act) and IDEA (1990) as "any item, piece of equipment, or product system, whether acquired commercially off-the-shelf, modified, or customized, that is used to increase, maintain or improve the functional capabilities of individuals with disabilities." It can describe both devices and services that aid an individual. The specific technology available may be limited to what the school or district has, but you can always request additional technology if you find it would benefit the student. In addition, the assistive technology specialist on your campus should be able to supply you with a wealth of information.

• •

Assistive technology specialist: Person who has knowledge of assistive technology, maintains technology devices, evaluates the devices, and trains people on how to use them.

• •

AT addresses students' needs in areas such as mobility, communication, positioning, independent living, adaptive toys, environmental access, leisure/recreation, seeing, and listening (Parette, 1998). AT devices are categorized along a continuum, ranging from no-tech to high-tech devices. No-tech options do not require equipment or devices (Lindsey, 2000), such as modifying the way that teaching is delivered to accommodate a particular child's unique needs, whereas low-tech devices include foam pencil grips, Velcro fasteners, adapted eating utensils, and other such solutions. High-tech devices are usually more sophisticated, including computers and systems that allow a person to control his environment. Parette (1998) noted that the factors that affect whether a particular AT device is deemed to be low-tech or high-tech include (a) cost, (b) transportability, (c) sophistication, (d) training required, (e) durability, (f) maintenance requirements, and (g) flexibility of use. Examples of AT devices are noted in Table 18.

Table 18

Examples of No-, Low-, and High-Tech Devices

No-Tech	Low-Tech	High-Tech
Providing services to the student from other service providers (e.g., occupational therapy, physical therapy).	Using adaptive switches that allow access for the student (e.g., electronic systems, battery-operated toys).	Incorporating the use of computers to aid the student with communication, recreation, or educational tasks.
Enlarging the size of print materials to make them easier to see.	Implementing call systems, such as loop tapes or buzzers, to communicate short messages.	Using devices with synthetic or digitized speech (also called *augmentative and alternative communication*).
Having the student sit in closer proximity to the teacher for hands-on instruction or to monitor behavior more closely.	Implementing notebooks, folders, or communication boards to communicate messages more appropriately.	Implementing powered mobility devices for a student to move about independently in the environment.
Having a peer assist a student who needs help performing specific tasks (e.g., writing, reading).	Stabilizing objects or activity frames with the use of elastic, Velcro, or other materials.	Using radio frequency, ultrasound, or infrared for environmental control systems.
Decreasing the number of test items, increasing test time, or both.	Using adapted books to facilitate participation in story time or reading.	Using advanced switches that detect eye or muscle movements.
Moving a student closer to her materials or closer to the chalkboard to help her see better.	Implementing adapted eating utensils to enable more effective self-feeding.	Using modified or alternative keyboards to give students access to computers.
Modifying the environment by removing visual stimuli and distracting sounds.	Using elongated levers for on/off switches or jigs for gross or fine motor control.	Implementing text-to-speech devices and Braille printers for access to information.

Note. From Bakken & Parette (2006).

• •

Assistive technology device: Any item, piece of equipment, or product system that is used to increase, maintain, or improve the functioning of individuals with disabilities. It may be purchased commercially off the shelf,
modified, or customized. The term does not include a medical device
that is surgically implanted, or the replacement of such a device.

• •

When assistive technology is considered for a student with certain learning
characteristics, careful attention must be given to ensure that the recommended assistive technology is required for the student to be successful and reflects
an appropriate match between the student and the tools (Zabala, 2002). For
example, given that prescription eyeglasses can be considered assistive technology, and that a certain degree of visual acuity is generally needed in order for an
individual to visually access print, one can see the importance of ensuring that
the prescription is appropriately matched to the visual needs of the individual.
If eyeglasses are arbitrarily assigned to an individual, they may serve as an ob-
stacle for the individual to see properly, thus hampering his overall performance.

There is much in the literature supporting using a team approach when considering the potential benefits of assistive technology for individuals (Brennan,
1998). A team approach is critical because no single individual will have all of
the necessary information to make decisions regarding appropriate assistive
technology (Smith, Benge, & Hall, 1994). Inge and Shepard (1995) indicated
that persons on decision-making teams should have knowledge of the potential
user of the assistive technology and his family, as well as a range of assistive
technology devices that may be deemed appropriate.

It is crucial that teams considering assistive technology for particular individuals be comprised of a variety of persons representing several aspects of
the student (Brennan, 1998). Stakeholders in this consideration process may
include the student for whom the assistive technology is being considered,
the student's family, the general education teacher(s), the special education
teacher(s), related services providers (e.g., speech-language pathologist, occupational therapist, physical therapist), school administrators, medical personnel, and rehabilitation counselors (Brennan, 1998) or a representative from a
vocational rehabilitation agency. The involvement of a variety of stakeholders
allows the team to consider multiple aspects of the student's abilities and needs
within multiple contexts, ultimately resulting in an appropriate match between
the student and the assistive technology and an ownership in the consideration
and implementation of the assistive technology amongst the team members.
Factors related to the consideration of assistive technology can be grouped into
the following domains: student, environment, tasks, and tools (Zabala, 2002).

· ·

Vocational rehabilitation agency: Provides a variety of services that focus on career development, employment preparation, achieving independence, and integration in the workplace and community for people with disabilities.

· ·

Consider the Student

As this process is a student-centered one, it makes sense that the first area to consider is the student. One goal of assistive technology is to capitalize on the ability of an individual to offset areas in which she has difficulties (Kelker & Holt, 2000). Therefore, it is necessary to determine the strengths that a person brings to the table in addition to her limitations (Melichair & Blackhurst, 1993). For instance, if a student in fifth grade has a good recall for information presented auditorily but has difficulty recalling information presented visually, then the team should note that auditory memory is his strength and eventually choose a tool that capitalizes on this strength. Questions such as "What does the student need to do?", "What are the student's current abilities?", and "What are the student's current needs?" (Zabala, 2002) should guide the assistive technology consideration process with respect to the student. The team should also consider the student's personal perceptions (i.e., preferences, expectations on the assistive technology, perceived need for potential assistive technology; Melichair & Blackhurst, 1993). How well the potential user of assistive technology "buys into" the consideration process and the potential assistive technology will have a large impact on whether or not the assistive technology will be successful (Rogers, 1995).

Consider Environmental Factors

It can be said that one's ability to perform is greatly dependent on what the environment will allow the student to do. An extreme example could be an individual's ability to access different levels in a building when the individual uses a wheelchair. If the building has an elevator or some other type of vertical access, then the individual is able to perform the task of moving well from floor to floor, whereas if the building only has stairs, then she will not be able to perform the task as well.

Perhaps a less obvious example would be the case of a student with Attention Deficit/Hyperactivity Disorder (ADHD). In a class that grouped all of the desks into islands, the student may be less attentive (because he is distracted by his peers) than if the desks were arranged in an alternate fashion. Zabala (2002) noted that materials currently available to the student, as well as potential supports, need to be considered across environments when evaluating for assistive technology. In looking at current materials and supports available, the team can identify potential tools and interventions that, if deemed to be appropriate, are readily available and may be easily implemented.

Readily available assistive technologies are those that are free and available to teachers. For example, your computer (both PC and Mac operating systems) comes with many assistive technologies already installed to help you and your students. It will be important as an inclusion teacher that you investigate these technologies to see if they will be appropriate for your students.

Environmental factors not only span across school contexts but contexts outside of school as well. In some cases, students will need to use the same assistive technology in the home setting that they use in the school setting. For example, a student who has difficulty recalling mathematical facts may use a calculator. It is likely that the calculator would be used on math-related problems within the school setting as well as for homework assignments. Consequently, factors related to the home life of the student should also be considered (Parette & Angelo, 1996; Parette & Brotherson, 1996). The team needs to determine the nature and extent of supports the student has outside of the school setting. Information related to the family's expectations, openness, and concerns regarding potential assistive technology needs to be accumulated and discussed.

Determine Which Tasks Will Be Affected

The third area of assistive technology consideration focuses on the tasks that the student is being asked to accomplish. This is first accomplished by surveying the activities that take place in the environment (Zabala, 2002). One could do this by observing the student, observing the student's peers, and interviewing the teacher to gain a picture of the tasks that the student is expected to perform. Then, one should determine which tasks are required of the student for progress toward mastery of an educational objective or for the student to be an active member of the class (Zabala, 2002). For example, consider a student who has visual perceptual difficulties in a fourth-grade math class. In observing the student, the student's peers, and interviewing the teacher, the following tasks might be noted: timed multiplication (2 digits by 1 digit) tests, preprinted worksheets, word problems, multiplication problem sets from the class text, multiplication practice at the board (i.e., problems are already written on the board and then the class discusses them), and flashcard drill and practice. It is noted in this student's IEP that he has grade-appropriate computation skills, but has difficulty lining up columns and often makes mistakes because he cannot keep his columns straight. In fact, a goal in his IEP states that he will successfully set up and solve mathematical problems. In looking at tasks that are needed for this student to successfully complete the goal, a team may determine to address all of the tasks except the flashcard drill and practice because all of the tasks require the student to either set up a mathematical problem and/or solve the problem while maintaining column order. In this way, tasks directly related to mastery of curricular and/or IEP goals are purposefully addressed.

Identify Appropriate Tools

Finally, tools should be identified that can be of use to the student across environments to support tasks. This phase occurs in four parts: (1) the identification of possible tools, (2) the evaluation of the tool characteristics for a best match, (3) the trial of the tools with the student, and (4) the acquisition of the tools for long-term use (Bowser & Reed, 1995; Edyburn, 2000; Zabala, 2002). When identifying tools, it is important to consider tools across the continuum from low-tech to high-tech (Zabala, 2002). Tools should be identified based on how they can augment a student's strengths, counterbalancing any effects of the student's disability, and/or how they can provide an alternate means of completing a task so as to circumnavigate the effects of the disability on the student's performance altogether (Lewis, 1993). Additionally, identification of tools should take into consideration previous tools either tried and discarded or tried and implemented.

The characteristics of the tools themselves are important in determining a best match between the tool and the student. King (1999) proposed four dimensions on which tool characteristics should be evaluated. The first dimension is the extent to which the tool places cognitive demands upon the student. Cognitive demands refer to the amount of thinking that is required to use a device. This may include sensing, remembering, discriminating, analyzing, and sequencing actions needed to operate the tool. The second dimension is the extent to which the tool places physical demands upon the student. Physical demands refer to the amount of muscle strength and movement required to initiate, pursue, and complete the task using the tool. Third, linguistic demands refer to the amount of symbolic interpretation and processing that the user must invest in order to operate the tool. Finally, time factors related to whether or not the tool will aid in the completion of the task within an acceptable amount of time need to be addressed. Other factors related to the characteristics of tools should include the tool's durability, dependability, lifespan, and maintenance costs/programs (Parette & Hourcade, 1997).

Assistive Technology for Reading

Reading is one of the major areas of difficulty that students may have in the inclusive classroom. Approximately 80% of students identified with learning disabilities (about half of all special education students) have their primary difficulties in reading (Lerner, 2002). Therefore, the likelihood is very good that you will have a student in your inclusive classroom who has reading difficulties.

Teachers can use computers that provide a multisensory delivery system for students with reading disabilities. Computers also allow the teacher to manipulate words, color-code them, and automatically link them with graphic cues, creating friendlier text for students to read. When writing is integrated with reading, "computers can offer students unlimited opportunities for practice and the repetition necessary to build fluency with continuous corrective feedback (computer-assisted instruction) and build comprehension by providing strategic prompts as students are reading/listening to content (e.g., eReader or ultimate Reader)" (Male, 2003, p. 48). Multimedia reading software also can provide additional practice or even another mode of instruction for students with reading problems. This software can include phonological decoding, reading comprehension, phonemic awareness, other emergent literacy issues, and "talking" storybooks (Ashton, 2000). Such technologies could provide students with extra time to practice skills and strategies learned in reading class and to apply them to more real-life situations while working on their use in more automatic ways (Bakken & Wojcik, 2004).

For students with reading and writing difficulties, a voice output or text-to-speech system may be useful. For example, an optical character recognition (OCR) system scans and converts written text into computer documents that can be read aloud by software (some of which is already built into computers' accessibility systems). Teachers can also use audiobooks or electronic books (eBooks) that can be downloaded online to help students with research and gathering information (Bakken & Wojcik, 2004). Most current children's books are available in both of these formats, and many classic texts can be found online free of charge to teachers. With the use of an OCR system with speech synthesis, text-to-speech software, or audiobooks, an individual with poor reading skills yet strong receptive oral language abilities is able to read and comprehend more easily. In addition, OCR systems allow students to directly input printed material into a computer and display it on the computer screen, which is helpful to students with print disabilities who can read more fluently in electronic format. Students could also use a handheld wand or pen such as the Quicktionary Pen (http://www.wizcomtech.com) to scan in single words or phrases that are then read aloud.

Assistive Technology for Writing

Students with learning difficulties can also experience problems with written expression. Struggling writers often have trouble getting their ideas written down fast enough (De La Paz & Graham, 1995), interfering with content generation and remembering ideas or text already planned in students' working memories. The ability to process information quickly can be a hindrance for many students. It has been noted that students often do not know the strategies for the writing process (Bakken & Whedon, 2003). Sometimes the actual act of handwriting limits the writing and creative abilities of these students.

Word processing software enables users to write without having to be overly concerned about making errors, releasing persons with written language deficits from worrying about the mechanics of writing and allowing them to redirect their efforts toward the meaning and content of their writing. Using the computer and various features of assistive software for writing makes the writing process easier, allows more writing to take place, and can ultimately boost the user's self-esteem (Bakken & Wojcik, 2004). Most word processing programs have voice output and both text-to-speech and speech-to-text capabilities, as well as spellcheckers, dictionaries and thesauruses, grammar checkers, and proofreading functions. Template-producing software provides forms and applications to make writing tasks easier and to facilitate brainstorming. Outlining programs enable the user to approach writing tasks by dumping his information into the program in an unstructured manner, then subsequently placing it into appropriate categories (Bakken & Wojcik, 2004).

Prewriting programs like webbing or concept-mapping applications are also beneficial to students with writing difficulties because they allow the user to diagram and make connections between ideas, creating an idea map that can be transformed into an outline, then to a draft paper, and finally a finished document. These types of software are particularly useful for students who have difficulty getting started, organizing, categorizing, sequencing, and polishing writing assignments (Bakken & Wojcik, 2004). Popular examples of these programs include Kidspiration and Inspiration (http://www.inspiration.com), as well as Draft:Builder 6 (http://www.donjohnston.com).

If students will be participating in classroom lectures and have problems keeping up, they can use tape-recorders, laptop computers, and pressure-sensitive paper for note taking. The Livescribe (http://www.livescribe.com) pen and paper system allows students to record lectures while taking notes. When students touch the pen to a particular word on the specialized paper, the pen will play back the parts of the lecture related to that specific notation. A student with strong auditory skills might try dictating his ideas onto a tape recorder and listening to it as a prewriting technique. In addition, materials produced by others (e.g., instructor materials, audiobooks) can be reviewed and read aloud to the user.

Reviewing Assistive Technologies

It is important to recognize that the process of considering assistive technology is ongoing and recursive (Bowser & Reed, 1995; Chambers, 1997; Melichair & Blackhurst, 1993; Zabala, 2002). Over time, it is conceivable that environments within which the student is expected to work will change. It must also be noted that simply getting or accessing assistive technology is not the only answer. The student must be taught how to use the assistive technology and how to implement it independently. In addition, as a student becomes older, the student's abilities, needs, expectations, and preferences may change, in turn affecting the match between the student, the tasks, and the tools (Melichair & Blackhurst, 1993). Furthermore, new technologies may become available that allow the student a greater degree of independence. Without periodic review, changes within the student, environment, tasks, and/or tools may be missed and the assistive technology system may be compromised.

Knowledge of Operating Systems

It is very important for teachers in inclusive environments to have knowledge about and experiences with multiple operating systems. This would include the Windows-based and Macintosh-based platforms. Although both platforms are similar and have similar capabilities, they also have some distinct differences.

You may not have a choice in what operating system you use, as the school that you will be teaching in may already have a certain platform that it is using. If this is the case, then you will need to look for software and applications that fit that particular format. If you are fortunate enough to be able to choose the platform that you use, then you will need to choose the format that best meets your students' learning needs and your teaching needs. Regardless of which platform you choose, as an inclusion teacher you should have experience with both formats and feel comfortable using either operating system.

Technology Training

Another area that inclusion teachers need to address is technology training. How can you use technology more efficiently? When is it appropriate to use technology? How can instruction be enhanced with the incorporation of technology? How can a student's needs be met using technology? The answers to these questions may come from classes you have taken in your teacher preparation program or they may need to be found. A good way to learn about technology is through training at the building level (e.g., training conducted by school staff or someone in the district), the district level (e.g., training conducted by someone in the district), or some other opportunity through an outside agency, university, or professional organization. Training can vary and what you become involved with may relate to your comfort level with the specific technology. There will be many different opportunities to learn about technology, as well as other important and relevant teacher topics, but it will be up to you to pursue finding out about and attending such training sessions in order to keep your knowledge and skills current.

Technology Support

The last area related to technology is that of support. What kind of support do you have in your building? What kind of support do you have in your district? If something goes wrong, then who will fix it? Is there someone to help you or do you need to learn how to do it yourself? Is there an internal support system in your building or school? If there is no or limited support, then you may want to pursue training that is focused more on how things operate and function. If you have access to more support, then your training may need to be more focused on the application of the technology. You will not be able to learn about everything because you also have to focus on yourself, your teaching, and your students. We recommend you make a list of everything you need to do, and then prioritize the list based on what resources you have access to and those that are not provided. This will enable you to make more of an educated decision and thus use the information you learn more directly and immediately, making a bigger impact on you and your students.

◇◇◇

SURVIVAL SECRETS OF TEACHERS

Julie, High School Special Education Teacher

What Is Your Current Position and How Long Have You Been Teaching?

Currently I teach in a high school setting in both inclusion and resource room classrooms. This is my third year as a special education teacher.

What Were Some of the Issues You Faced With Technology as a First-Year Teacher?

One of the biggest issues I faced was that I was unfamiliar with Apple computers. In my high school we have both formats (PC and Mac) and some teachers use one and some the other. My students were in classes that used some of each, so I needed to be able to work with both formats. Because my teacher preparation training was only on a PC, I was at a disadvantage when it came to the use and functions of the Mac computer. This disadvantage was transferred to my students in that I could not help them as much as I wanted on work that involved a Mac. The other issue I had was with assistive technology. I had very little training in this area and did not really understand what it was. I didn't know it could range from low-tech to high-tech and everything in between. I had no idea of all of the assistive technologies available to students to help them with their learning and to make materials accessible to them. I also was not aware that many of these assistive technologies are free or come already installed on most computers.

How Did You Deal With Any Deficits in the Area of Technology?

First, I enrolled in workshops and in-services that addressed Mac computers. I also contacted teachers in my building and the district technology personnel to seek advice and training. I also enrolled in a class on assistive technology at a nearby university. This gave me the background knowledge that I needed. I also researched assistive technology and attended sessions at conferences I attended. I knew that I must be proactive and seek out this knowledge to meet the learning and behavioral needs of my students.

What Advice Would You Give Future Teachers About Technology?

My advice would be to never stop learning. Technology will be a major factor in students' learning. Take technology classes, experience technology, research technology, and be open to technology. Technology isn't always the saving grace. Just like anything else, it can serve a specific purpose and function. Don't just use technology to use it. Develop your lesson plans accordingly and when technology is appropriate then implement it. Also consider assistive technology for students. Sometimes this technology will be the only thing that allows students to communicate or participate with other students. Technology can be powerful so be open to it and learn about it.

Conclusion

Teachers in inclusive classrooms must also be aware of the different types of assistive technologies available to their students. First, teachers must be aware of what assistive technology is, how it can be implemented with students, and the process of deciding which technology will be the most effective in the inclusion classroom. Next, teachers need to understand the two basic operating systems, what each has to offer, and how they function so they are able to use either in their classroom. Third, if teachers lack some technology skills, then they will need to seek out professional development opportunities to remediate their deficiencies. Finally, teachers should be aware of what supports are in place within their school and district for technology assistance. Teaching is a profession that is constantly changing and evolving. In order to keep up with the changes and be as effective as possible, teachers in inclusive classrooms need to be cognizant of technological expectations and how important they are to students, parents, and other school personnel.

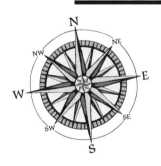

Survival Tips

- Take advantage of any technology that the school is willing to provide for your classroom and be willing to learn how to use it.

- Many students come to your classroom knowing a great deal about technology. Let them use their technology skills to complete assignments and projects and practice new academic skills. Technology can increase academic engagement.

- Most school districts have a technology support specialist who can assist you in acquiring new software programs for your students. She may also be able to provide training for you and your students.

Survival Toolkit

Websites to Support You With Technology

- Assistive Technology in Education: A Guide for the Delivery of Assistive Technology Services for Students with Disabilities: http://www.atp.ne.gov/techassistdoc.html

- Education World: Assistive Technology: http://www.educationworld.com/special_ed/assistive/index.shtml

- Family Village School: Assistive Technology for Students with Disabilities: http://www.familyvillage.wisc.edu/education/at.html

- National Assistive Technology in Education Network: http://www.natenetwork.org

○ Assistive Technology Resources: http://www.parentpals.com/gossamer/pages/Assistive_Technology/index.html

Books to Support You With Technology

Besnoy, K. D., & Clarke, L. W. (Eds.). (2010). *High-tech teaching success!* Waco, TX: Prufrock Press.

Brooks-Young, S. (2010). *Teaching with the tools kids really use: Learning with web and mobile technologies.* Thousand Oaks, CA: Corwin.

Fitzgibbon, K. (2010). *Teaching with wikis, blogs, podcasts & more: Dozens of easy ideas for using technology to get kids excited about learning.* New York, NY: Scholastic.

Green, J. L. (2011). *The ultimate guide to assistive technology in special education: Resources for education, intervention, and rehabilitation.* Waco, TX: Prufrock Press.

Mills, S. C., & Roblyer, M. D. (2006). *Technology tools for teachers: A Microsoft Office tutorial* (2nd ed.). Upper Saddle River, NJ: Prentice Hall.

Richardson, W. (2010). *Blogs, wikis, podcasts, and other powerful Web tools for classrooms* (3rd ed.). Thousand Oaks, CA: Corwin.

Sharp, V. F. (2009). *Computer education for teachers: Integrating technology into classroom teaching* (6th ed.). Hoboken, NJ: Wiley.

10 Placement Options for Inclusive and Special Education Teachers

One of the benefits of being a special education teacher is that you will have many opportunities to teach in a variety of settings. Often, teachers feel that they have to accept the first teaching position they are offered and may not be aware of the options available to them. Although most schools provide inclusive classrooms for students with disabilities, federal mandates require schools to offer a continuum of services. Therefore, you may be teaching in a resource room or a self-contained classroom depending on your teacher training and qualifications. This chapter is going to consider several of the jobs in which teachers trained in inclusive and special education may find themselves. We've elected to place it as the last chapter of this book because you may find yourself choosing to switch positions during your career as a teacher as new opportunities arise.

If you are a teacher with special education certification, you are in a position to take some time to research job openings before making a decision. There are schools throughout the U.S. that have special education teaching positions filled by uncertified teachers or left vacant each year because of lack of personnel (Thornton, Peltier, & Medina, 2007). There continues to be a shortage of qualified teachers throughout the field of special education.

Although a school is governed by the rules and regulations of the district, it also has a great deal of latitude in the way the special education program is set up. This site-based management approach makes it necessary to look at each school's program individually. When looking at job postings, research the district and the school's website. If possible, talk to some of the teachers who work in the school district and at the school where you are considering taking a teaching position.

Most importantly, do not take a teaching position if it does not match your qualifications or experience. Because of special education teacher shortages in many states, the principal may be anxious to place you in a classroom just to fill the position. For example, if you are trained to work with students who have learning disabilities, you should strongly evaluate whether or not you are qualified to take a position in a self-contained classroom for students with severe emotional disabilities. This is not fair to you or the students. A special education classroom is not an on-the-job training site for a special education teacher. Students with disabilities have unique academic, social, emotional, and, sometimes, medical needs and they deserve to be taught by a well-trained professional.

As a special education teacher, you also need to consider the types of teaching arrangements that are available in many special education programs. The next section will provide an overview of each of these arrangements and what your roles and responsibilities may include within that arrangement.

The Inclusive Classroom

Since the 1990 reauthorization of IDEA, schools have slowly begun increasing the number of students with disabilities served in the general education classroom. According to the National Center for Education Statistics (2006), 53.7% of students with disabilities spent more than 79% of their time in the general education classroom due to the expansion of inclusion. An inclusive classroom is made up of students with and without disabilities. The number of students with disabilities placed in each general education classroom is going to vary across classes. The lead teacher of the classroom will be a general education teacher, but the special education teacher will provide support to students with disabilities within the classroom. There are obvious challenges to this arrangement for both teachers and students, but it has been met with great success throughout many classrooms. You may also hear the term *push-in*, meaning the teacher goes into the classroom to serve the students.

First of all, effective inclusion requires planning. The general education teacher and the special education teacher will work together to decide how to teach the content to all of the students in the classroom. The general education teacher should be certified in the content area (or in general elementary education) and know the curriculum requirements for that particular course. The special education teacher should have a great deal of knowledge regarding evidence-based practices and effective teaching strategies that will benefit all students. This is not to say that the general education teacher does not already use best practices, but that the special education teacher is familiar with all disability areas and knows the impact of those disabilities on the academic functioning of students with an identified disability. Therefore, meeting together for planning purposes is essential to providing a healthy inclusive environment.

Secondly, scheduling is probably one of the most challenging issues for all teachers but can be exceptionally difficult for the special education teacher who needs to be in two places at one time. For example, you may have a caseload of 15 students, and you have to work with each student within his general education classroom over the course of the week. This requires collaboration from each teacher or related service provider who serves the student. Meeting as a team is the most effective way to set up a schedule that works for everyone and will be necessary to plan out the most efficient use of your time.

It may also be possible to meet with your school principal prior to beginning the school year to assist in developing the class schedules of your students with disabilities so that you can be in the classroom with each student at the appropriate time. When talking with the principal, share with him the importance of not only providing support to the students but also to their general education teachers, who will be much more effective in their classrooms if you are able to provide support to your students at a specified time.

Providing support in an inclusive classroom can be a very positive experience for both you and the students, but it does come with its own set of challenges. Many teachers are often placed in an inclusive classroom without any training in how to teach in that setting. Therefore, your responsibilities within the inclusive classroom may look very different depending on the principal's philosophy, as well as the general education teacher's philosophy. It will be important to discuss inclusion with the principal prior to the beginning of the school year to have a better understanding of the expectations of the position. Once you find out that you will be teaching in an inclusive classroom, plan to meet with the general education teacher and spend some time discussing each of your specific roles and responsibilities within that setting.

SURVIVAL SECRETS OF TEACHERS

Lydia, Inclusion Specialist

What Is Your Current Position and How Long Have You Been Teaching?

I am currently teaching as an elementary inclusion teacher for third and fourth grades, and I just completed my second year of teaching. I work in three third-grade classes and three fourth-grade classes.

Why Did You Accept the Position as an Inclusion Specialist?

During my time in college, we spent a lot of time talking about different positions that we could teach in, and I felt that teaching in inclusive classrooms was the wave of the future for teaching. I also have a minor in math, and I know how difficult content can be. The schools in my area all push for full inclusion, so they want to hire teachers who are comfortable in that type of setting. It's a good fit for me.

What Do You Like Most About Your Job?

I like that I have to know a lot about disability areas and think beyond just the disability itself. It is my responsibility to figure out how students with disabilities can be the most successful in the general education classroom. That requires me to know a great deal about research-based practices and make educational decisions on the strategies that would be most effective for my students. I also feel that I learn a lot from the general education teachers. I try to understand the challenges of having students with disabilities in their classroom and how I can support the teacher as well as the students.

What Are Some of the Challenges of Working in an Inclusive Classroom?

Scheduling and planning! Both can be challenging at best, but trying to make sure that I am in the right place at the right time is not always easy. Throw in IEP meetings, special events, Friday fun days, holidays, and so on, and I worry that I'm not meeting the requirements of the IEP. Fortunately, I am invited to the grade-level team meetings for planning, but my schedule makes it difficult to attend on a consistent basis. I don't really have time to write lesson plans for six classes, but when I attend the meetings, I have time to plan ways to teach the content so that my students can be successful. I also know that the general education teachers appreciate the effort I make to attend the meetings.

What Advice Would You Give Someone Considering a Position as an Inclusion Specialist?

Be flexible! If you like a typical classroom setting where you have your own desk and your own students, this may not be the position for you. You have to be a good collaborator, a good listener, an organizer, and a lifelong learner. Each teacher is different so the way you handle students from one class may be very different than the way you handle students from another class. To be effective and efficient, it is important that you communicate on a regular basis with the general education teacher about the students. It is also important to develop positive working relationships with the general education teachers and follow through on your responsibilities. If you can develop positive relationships, then the general education teachers will appreciate all that you do in their classroom.

The Resource Classroom

In a resource classroom, students receive some of their instruction within the general education classroom but will leave the classroom for extra instructional support from a special education teacher in another classroom. For example, students may remain in the general education classroom for the majority of instruction, but go to the resource room for extra assistance in reading. This is known as a pull-out program. Due to the increased adoption of inclusion, this is not a placement option found in many schools.

Scheduling, as discussed previously, will be a critical component for ensuring that all students receive the amount of support required by their IEP. The benefits of this arrangement may be a smaller class size with specialized instruction. At the same time, students with disabilities may feel stigmatized in having to leave the general education classroom and go to another location for instruction. Whether or not to serve the student within the general education classroom or have the student come to the resource classroom is an IEP decision.

IDEA (2004) also requires that students be provided access to the general education curriculum. As a resource teacher, you will need to work closely with the general education teachers in developing your lesson plans so that students are receiving the same content. Because students will be coming in and out of your classroom throughout the day, organization and planning is essential. Resource teachers often have to be familiar with the content in more than one grade level, and trying to attend grade-level team meetings can be difficult when they are held at the same time that you have students coming to your room for instruction. For more information on the lesson planning process, refer to Chapter 5, Planning Academic Instruction.

SURVIVAL SECRETS OF TEACHERS

Debra, High School Resource Teacher

What Is Your Current Position and How Long Have You Been Teaching?

I am currently a high school resource teacher for 9th and 10th grade, and this is my third year of teaching.

Why Did You Accept the Position to Teach in a Resource Classroom?

To be honest, I really needed a job, and this was the only one that I was offered when I graduated from college. I was afraid I might not be offered another position, but it was a good decision because I really like teaching in a resource classroom.

What Do You Like Most About Your Job?

Every day is different. I have the opportunity to work with a lot of students who seem to use my classroom as a place of respite. I think high school can be overwhelming for students with disabilities and having a room to come to where they can get specialized help without any of their general education peers looking on seems to reduce the anxiety for some of my students. I also enjoy getting to know most of the teachers. I try to have a good collaborative relationship with them, so that we can work together and do what's best for the students. The position can definitely be challenging, but that's one of the things I like most about it.

What Are Some of the Challenges of Working in a Resource Classroom?

Sometimes I feel like I have to be all things to all students, and that's not possible. When students come to my room, they feel comfortable enough to share their ups and downs of the day. I listen, but I sometimes find it difficult to get them to focus on their schoolwork. It can also be challenging to keep up with the paperwork for all of the students on my caseload and, at the same time, make sure I have well-developed lesson plans for two grade levels and a variety of content areas.

What Advice Would You Give Someone Considering a Position in a Resource Classroom?

Be well organized but flexible. When you're working with multiple grade levels, you have to work around schedules for both students and teachers. If organizational skills are not one of your strengths, this might not be the job for you. You also have to get along well with teachers. Students are leaving their classroom and coming to yours, so you have to respect teachers' time but also make sure you are serving the student within the resource classroom for the required amount of time as written in the IEP.

◇◇◇

The Self-Contained Classroom

In a self-contained classroom, students receive all of their instruction within that classroom. The students within this setting typically have more significant behavioral, physical, and/or mental challenges. The students may leave the classroom for brief periods of time throughout the day, but the majority of instruction is provided in the self-contained classroom. Planning academic instruction can be challenging because of the varying levels of academic functioning within the classroom. Along with academics, you may also be implementing a number of behavior plans, so knowing how to design and implement behavior plans will be important. One of the benefits to teaching in this setting is that the same students remain in the classroom all day. You may be able to identify your students' strengths and areas of need sooner than if you saw them for a limited amount of time each day.

Because students who are served in a self-contained classroom tend to have more significant disabilities, you need to make sure that you have the knowledge and the expertise to work in this setting. In addition, you will be working with other professionals who serve these students within your classroom, so collaboration will be necessary in planning for each student.

Depending on the number of students placed in your classroom, you will have at least one instructional aide. Each state has a required ratio of instructional aides to students in a self-contained classroom, and you should find out what that ratio is from the special education director. Too often, the principal will overload a classroom beyond what is allowed, and this will have a negative impact on you, the instructional aides, and your students. Working closely with your special education director will help you avoid this problem, but if this situation cannot be resolved, your recourse is to contact the special education office at the state level for support. Figure 19 provides a list of questions that you should ask when considering a position in a self-contained setting.

- How many students will be in the class?
- What is the limit on class size?
- What are the disability areas of the students?
- What are the ages of the students?
- How many instructional aides will be working with the students?
- What will the role of the instructional aide(s) be?
- At what level is each of the students included in the general education classroom?
- What related service providers work with the students?

Figure 19. Questions to ask about self-contained placements.

SURVIVAL SECRETS OF TEACHERS

Emily, Teacher in a Self-Contained Classroom

What Is Your Current Position?

I just completed my second year in a self-contained classroom for students with moderate to severe intellectual disabilities (ID), autism, Down syndrome, Fragile X syndrome, and cerebral palsy. I teach in a high school with about 1,900 students in a small town in North Carolina.

Why Did You Accept the Position to Teach in a Self-Contained Classroom?

I took a job in a self-contained classroom because I wanted a small group of students all day that I could teach and hopefully impact in a positive way. In other settings, teachers have larger class sizes and at least three different classes a day.

What Do You Like Most About Your Job?

I enjoy being able to teach academic skills, functional skills, vocational skills, and self-help skills. There is a lot of flexibility on what my lesson plans consist of. Also, by having the same students all day I get to know them really well. I also enjoy being able to go on field trips with my students regularly. We go to the grocery store once a month to buy the ingredients we need for cooking class, and we usually go on at least one other outing a month. We have taken the students to plays, local businesses, the police department, the fire department, and the zoo. The students really gain a lot of experience by going on these field trips. As high school students, it is very important that they understand how to act properly in a social setting and what to expect when they are in public. We use social stories and practice appropriate behavior before going on each field trip, and the students usually surprise me with how well they behave.

I also enjoy working in a high school because it gives my students access to different types of classes. We have a number of teachers who open up their classes and planning times to work with my students. One of the general education P.E. teachers loves to bring her class into my students' P.E. time and work with them. They even organize a field day for my students every year run by general education students. The dance teacher allows us to come in every other week during her planning time and teaches the students dance elements and a collaborative routine they perform during their winter and spring concerts. Other teachers have donated items to our students, and most teachers take time to talk to my students every day. I work in a supportive school with a lot of great people.

What Are Some of the Challenges in Working in a Self-Contained Classroom?

There are many challenges I face in my classroom each day. Because of the lower cognitive level of some of the students, their behavior can be very unpredictable, and they can sometimes be aggressive. Another challenge in teaching students in a high school self-contained setting is the possibility that the student may remain in the same class for 8 years. This is because these students have a right to a public education until the age of 21 (or 22 depending on their birthday). I think teaching the same students for a long period of time may not be in their best interest. As teachers, I think there is the potential for us to become too comfortable and complacent with our students, and as a result, we may not be as effective in challenging our students over a long period of time.

What Advice Would You Give Someone Considering a Position in a Self-Contained Classroom?

If you are considering a position as a self-contained teacher make sure you ask lots of questions during your interview process. Ask about the disabilities of the students you are going to be teaching, their level of performance, and what kinds of behaviors the students display. You also need to know if there is any lifting you will have to do for students in wheelchairs. This may or may not be something you are able to do. One of the things I did that I found helpful was to observe the classroom I would be teaching in before I accepted the position. This gave me a lot of insight on what to expect, and I was able to plan things over the summer with the specific students in mind.

◇◇

The Co-Taught Classroom

Many students are now being served in an inclusive setting where a general education teacher and a special education teacher co-teach. This involves the sharing of roles and responsibilities by two licensed teachers in the classroom. This does not mean that one of the teachers assumes the role of teacher and the other assumes the role of a paraprofessional. Both teachers are engaged in teaching. There are several ways to implement co-teaching. Friend and Cook (2007) described the following six models of co-teaching:

1. *One Teach—One Observe.* One teacher provides the instruction, while the other teacher observes a student, a group of students, or the entire class.
2. *One Teach—One Assist.* One teacher provides the instruction, while the other teacher moves around the classroom, providing individual assistance as needed.
3. *Station Teaching.* Both teachers provide instruction, while students move around the classroom to stations. Sometimes, one station is set aside for peer tutoring, homework, or independent work.
4. *Parallel Teaching.* Both teachers plan the instruction, while each teacher then teaches half of the class at the same time.
5. *Alternative Teaching.* One teacher may provide small-group instruction, while the other teacher provides instruction to the whole class.
6. *Teaming.* Both teachers are responsible for planning and instruction for all of the students in the class.

Successful co-teaching requires ongoing professional development for the teachers, collaboration between the teachers, a joint planning time, and administrative support. This can be a challenging teaching role if you do not take the time to address some of the key issues prior to the first day of class. Co-teaching is becoming a more common service delivery approach because it addresses the diversity of the students' needs within the general education classroom. It also reduces the instructional fragmentation that can occur in more traditional classrooms when students are constantly leaving the classroom to receive services in another part of the building (Friend & Cook, 2007).

Many co-teachers will describe their relationship as a "professional marriage." There are some challenging issues that have to be discussed to build a successful partnership as co-teachers. Co-teaching requires a willingness to change teaching styles and preferences, share responsibilities, and work closely with another adult while relying on another individual in order to perform tasks previously done alone (Friend & Cook, 2007).

Understanding each other's philosophy of education and teaching is essential in building a strong working relationship. Figure 20 provides a comprehensive list of issues that you and your co-teacher should discuss prior to the beginning of the school year. This will give you the opportunity to develop a plan that works for both of you, thus increasing the likelihood of a positive co-teaching experience. Investing some time to discuss these important issues may help alleviate the stress that can be involved in sharing a classroom and all of the responsibilities that are part of that teaching position.

SURVIVAL SECRETS OF TEACHERS

Golda, Teacher in a Co-Taught Classroom

What Is Your Current Position and How Long Have You Been Teaching?

I am a middle school special education teacher at an alternative school for students who need small class sizes in a self-contained setting. I just completed my first year and I taught English, history, civics, and life science. This summer, I am co-teaching literacy in summer school.

Why Did You Accept the Position to Teach in a Co-Taught Classroom?

I accepted a position to teach in a co-taught classroom because I learned from my first year that there is a lot about teaching that I still need to learn. Managing behavior is by far my biggest challenge. It helps me to see how other special education teachers respond to adolescents in a way that is appropriate to their disability. When I found out that one of my colleagues would be teaching reading this summer and I had an opportunity to work with and learn from her, I took the position right away so that I could be better prepared for challenges I foresee in my second year.

Preparation and Planning for Co-Teaching	
Philosophical Beliefs	
Educational philosophies	
Challenges for giving up control	
Non-negotiables regarding your teaching role	
Classroom Environment	
Physical arrangement (student and teacher's desks)	
Noise level	
Blackboard	
Bulletin boards	
Computers	
Classroom Management	
Classroom rules	
Addressing discipline issues	
Routines and procedures	
Instructional Issues	
Developing lesson plans	
Lecture	
Small groups (peer tutoring)	
Activities/projects	
Homework	
Grading/report cards	
Collaboration	
Developing good communication skills	
Maintaining a professional relationship	
Delineation of roles and responsibilities	
Addressing professional disagreements	
External Supports	
Administrative support	
Professional development	

Figure 20. Preparation and planning for co-teaching.

What Do You Like Most About Your Job?

What I like most about co-teaching is learning from and collaborating with my colleague. She has taught me a lot about finding resources that make our content more accessible to students. For example, because we teach literacy under the theme of geography, she has found text from all over the world in print, digital, and audio copies. I have benefitted a lot from her research, and now I know of resources I can access that go beyond the scope of most teacher websites and books. I also appreciate how I have been able to apply her behavior management techniques to my experiences with students. Because managing behavior is my biggest challenge, it helps to learn from her example, and now I am in a better position to anticipate and respond effectively to disruptive behavior. One of the most beneficial aspects of co-teaching is having another teacher around so we can support each other when students engage in disruptive behavior, and one of us may have to leave the classroom to handle a situation. I also think having more than one teacher in the classroom helps keep students on task and everyone benefits from a smoothly run classroom.

What Are Some of the Challenges of Working in a Co-Taught Classroom?

Any time people collaborate, I think there is always a challenge in the division of labor. Sometimes, one teacher has an interest in teaching a particular unit, and it can be difficult to know how to split the workload with your co-teacher. You want to make sure both teachers have a sense of ownership and mastery of the material, but at times, you want to just take charge because it seems less time consuming and more efficient. My colleague and I are very sensitive to each other, and we double check with one another by meeting in our spare time to plan and avoid these types of conflict. In class, we also try not to undermine one another's authority, but that is also much easier said than done. In reality, we do make mistakes in and out of the classroom, but we try to communicate often so we can acknowledge our challenges and try to avoid them in the future.

What Advice Would You Give Someone Considering a Position in a Co-Taught Classroom?

I would tell someone considering a position in a co-taught classroom that it is a very rewarding experience. The challenges of collaborating with another educator are difficult, but the best way to look at it is to approach the job with humility. I think my colleague and I have a great relationship, because we are more considerate of the students' educational well-being than our own pride. When I observe other teachers having difficulty in co-teaching situations, it is usually because one or both of them takes a conflict too far. They don't stop and sit down and talk about the problem immediately, and as a result, the students are the ones who suffer the most. In short, I would remind anyone who co-teaches not to lose sight of why they teach and to do the right thing in the best interest of the students, even when it's difficult.

◇◇

Other Placement Options

Special education and inclusion teachers are not always assigned to a specific classroom. Some school districts hire itinerant teachers who may work at more than one school. For example, teachers who are working as consultants, behavior specialists, or physical disabilities specialists may travel between schools because of the low number of students they will be serving at each school. The most challenging aspect of this position is scheduling. You have to be aware of each school's schedule, as well as the students' classroom schedules, to make sure that you meet the time requirements of each IEP.

Job Satisfaction

Obviously, teaching any student takes a great deal of commitment and a high energy level, but teaching students with disabilities can be even more challenging because of the additional responsibilities that are included with this population of students (e.g., writing IEPs, planning and attending IEP meetings, developing behavioral intervention plans). Research studies have shown that there are certain key factors that increase the rate of burnout for teachers working with students with disabilities no matter what the setting. You need to know what those factors are, and if possible, address some of those issues before you accept a position.

Although teachers with a special education background bring a great deal of expertise to a school, your job can also leave you feeling isolated and overwhelmed. Unlike general education teachers who make up the majority of the teachers at the school, you may be one of a few special education teachers or in some cases, the only special education teacher in the school. Furthermore, if you are teaching in inclusive classrooms, you are balancing additional content, grading, and team meetings (to name a few) in addition to all of your other responsibilities as a special education teacher.

In a 2007 study, Gehrke and McCoy identified factors that were related to job satisfaction for special education teachers whether in an inclusive setting or a more self-contained setting. These included support of welcoming colleagues, a special education mentor, a network of support, adequate materials to support teaching practices, and relevant professional development opportunities. Based on these findings, it would be in your best interest to ask questions regarding these factors prior to accepting a teaching position.

Research has also shown that teachers who are familiar with the process and procedures and have supports and resources in place are more likely to continue working in the field of special education. An analysis of the responses of 1,153 special education teachers who had been teaching for fewer than 5 years indicated that "school districts need to provide systematic and responsive teacher induction programs for all beginning special educators" (Billingsley, Carlson, & Klein, 2004, p. 345). There should be a separate orientation process specifically designed for this group of teachers. Although the primary goal for both special education teachers and general education teachers is student success, special education teachers have a specific set of roles and responsibilities that are unique to their position. Because these roles and responsibilities can vary widely across schools, it is important that you attend this induction program with each special education position you accept.

In a 2006 study, Plash and Piotrowski explored the retention issues of 70 highly qualified special education teachers in Alabama. Results showed that the two most important criteria contributing to their decision to leave the field were excessive paperwork and stress created by demands of the job. These findings were consistent with Gersten, Keating, and Yovanoff (2001), who found that stress from the demanding responsibilities affected attrition and retention. According to Gersten et al., teachers believe they are hired to teach children with disabilities, when in reality they spend the vast part of their day completing paperwork and attending meetings. This information is not included to scare you away from the field, but to better prepare you for some of the challenges you will face. Knowledge is power, and knowing what questions to ask when you are searching for jobs will assist you in finding the job and school that is the right match for you.

Conclusion

Whether you are brand new to teaching or considering a change in your career placement, understanding the different options for employment in inclusive and special education is vital in order to find the correct match for your abilities. In addition, you may find yourself working with individuals teaching in these varied settings, so it's important to understand what their job responsibilities entail.

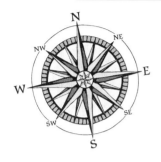

Survival Tips

- Bring a list of questions that are important to you to the job interview; this shows prospective employers that you are prepared for and thoughtful about your career.

- When you are unable to attend team or grade-level meetings, ask if someone can take notes for you.

- Learn from your colleagues. Experienced teachers can answer questions, provide suggestions, solve problems, and provide support and encouragement.

Survival Toolkit

Websites to Support You With Inclusion and Placement Options

- What is Inclusion?: http://www.kidstogether.org/inclusion.htm

- Special Education Inclusion: http://www.weac.org/Issues_Advocacy/Resource_Pages_On_Issues_One/Special_Education/special_education_inclusion.aspx

- Special Education Placement: http://school.familyeducation.com/special-education/ada/38441.html

- The Inclusion Classroom: http://techinclusion.tripod.com

- Inclusion of Students with Special Needs: Teaching and Learning: http://www.marthalakecov.org/~building/spneeds/inclusion/teaching/front_teaching.html

Books to Support You With Inclusion and Placement Options

Boon, R. T., & Spencer, V. G. (Eds.). (2010). *Best practices for the inclusive classroom: Scientifically based strategies for success.* Waco, TX: Prufrock Press.

Gargiulo, R. M. (2012). *Special education in contemporary society: An introduction to exceptionality* (4th ed.). Thousand Oaks, CA: SAGE Publications.

Hallahan, D. P., Kauffman, J. M., & Pullen, P. C. (2009). *Exceptional learners: An introduction to special education* (11th ed.). Boston, MA: Allyn & Bacon.

Smith, D. D., & Tyler, N. C. (2010). *Introduction to special education: Making a difference* (7th ed.). Upper Saddle River, NJ: Merrill.

Closing Thoughts

Over the last 20 years, U.S. schools have gone through many demographic changes. Nearly half of all students in public schools (42%) are students of color and approximately 20% of students speak a language other than English at home (Voltz & Collins, 2010). About 14% have identified disabilities (U.S. Department of Education, 2007a). Of those with disabilities, about half spend 80% or more of the school day in general education classrooms (U.S. Department of Education, 2007b). Given this information, most classrooms are highly diverse. This obviously has an enormous impact on teacher training programs and how we prepare special education teachers.

In the past, general education teachers tended to work in independent classrooms with homogeneous populations because students with disabilities were segregated into other classrooms or buildings. Fortunately, federal mandates and societal views have sought to change that traditional pattern and classrooms are now opening their doors to a wide variety of learners (Slobodzian, 2009). Therefore, a majority of special education teachers are spending most of their time in the general education classroom and can often feel as though they have to be a "jack of all trades." That's not possible! Although the special education teacher brings expertise regarding the academic and behavioral skills of students with disabilities to the inclusive classroom setting, the general education teacher has expertise in the content area and teaching skills for students functioning approximately at grade level. Thus, classrooms require the expertise of both types of educators. However, that does not mean that all special educators will be placed in an inclusive classroom.

In 1995, Fuchs and Fuchs published an article titled "What's 'Special' About Special Education? A Field Under Siege." In this article, the authors suggested that special education is special because of its unique resources, its impact on student performance, and the effectiveness of teaching practices that are implemented by highly trained teachers. Some of these teaching practices are validated by special educators, but do not easily transfer to the inclusive classroom setting. Congressional sponsors of IDEA recognized that the inclusive classroom may not be capable of providing an appropriate education to all students, and thus developed a continuum of alternative placements. Your teaching career may begin in one of these alternative placements, but if you remain in the field of special education for very long, it is likely that you will have the opportunity to teach in an inclusive classroom. Therefore, it is our recommendation that all special educators be prepared to teach in inclusive settings.

Teaching for Success

All of the book's authors have taught as special educators in K–12 education and searched our own prior knowledge and experience as teachers to pinpoint the type of information that would be necessary for you to begin your teaching career. First of all, we know the importance of collaboration and communication. Both of these skills are essential in working in schools. Because the foundation of special education is the IEP, your job involves working with a number of other teachers, administrators, related service personnel, and parents but can certainly move beyond this scope. Underlying the IEP are the federal mandates that ensure that students with disabilities are provided with a free and appropriate public education. You will need to be able to communicate the intent of these laws and explain how they support the decisions that are made by the IEP team.

One of your primary responsibilities will be to develop lesson plans and provide academic instruction for students with disabilities. This will often be within the context of the general education classroom. Information from the IEP, such as accommodations and modifications, will certainly assist you in developing those plans, but knowing how to assess student progress and manage classroom behavior are essential skills for all teachers. Furthermore, you will also be able to use research-based instructional strategies alongside the general education teacher. These strategies will benefit all students in the classroom.

As you read through each of these chapters, we discussed the issue of documentation and data collection several times. Much of this can now be done through the use of technology. Technology can be used to write the IEP, document student progress (academic and behavioral), document communications regarding the student (e.g., to parents, with other teachers), develop lesson plans, and even implement instruction. In addition, students are also using technology on a daily basis both inside and outside of the classroom. It can often be frustrating for teachers when you are using an outdated computer or do not have access to the most up-to-date programs that are available. Most districts provide technology support for their teachers, so remaining current on the technologies that are available will enable you to know what resources to request for data management or instructional purposes.

Being a Lifelong Learner

You will not know everything there is to know your first year of teaching. No one does. Expert teachers have years of experience and have learned from their successes and their mistakes. Take advantage of the experience other teachers have to offer, but you also need to continue your professional education. With the ever-changing field of special education, it is imperative that you stay current on research and legislation. Taking college courses, reading professional journals, and attending professional development trainings will help you continue expanding your own skills as a special educator. In the end, your students will reap the benefits.

References

Americans with Disabilities Act of 1990, Pub. L. No. 101–336.

Ashton, T. M. (2000). Technology for students with learning disabilities in reading. *Journal of Special Education, 15*(2), 47–48.

Bakken, J. P., & Parette, P. (2006). Using technology to advance multicultural special education. In F. E. Obiakor (Ed.), *Multicultural special education* (pp. 272–289). Upper Saddle River, NJ: Merrill-Prentice Hall.

Bakken, J. P., & Whedon, C. K. (2003). Giving students with learning disabilities the POWER to write: Improving the quality and quantity of written products. *Learning Disabilities: A Multidisciplinary Journal, 12,* 13–22.

Bakken, J. P., & Wojcik, B. W. (2004). Technology resources for persons with learning disabilities. In F. E. Obiakor & A. F. Rotatori (Eds.), *Advances in special education: Current perspectives on learning disabilities* (Vol. 16, pp. 113–132). Oxford, England: Elsevier/JAI.

Billingsley, B., Carlson, E., & Klein, S. (2004). Working conditions and induction support of early career special educators. *Exceptional Children, 70,* 333–347.

Bloom, L. A., Hursh, D., Wienke, W. D., & Wold, R. K. (1992). The effects of computer assisted data collection on students' behaviors. *Behavioral Assessment, 14,* 173–190.

Boardman, A. G., Arguelles, M. E., Vaughn, S., Hughes, M. T., & Klingner, J. (2005). Special education teachers' views of research-based practices. *Journal of Special Education, 39,* 168–180.

Bowser, G., & Reed, P. (1995). Education TECH points for assistive technology planning. *Journal of Special Education Technology, 12,* 325–338.

Brennan, J. K. (1998). Assistive technology: It takes a team. *The Delta Kappa Gamma Bulletin, 64*(2), 24–28.

Brimijoin, K. (2002). *A journey toward expertise in differentiation: A preservice and inservice teacher make their way.* Unpublished doctoral dissertation. University of Virginia, Charlottesville.

Brimijoin, K., Marquissee, E., & Tomlinson, C. A. (2003). Using data to differentiate instruction. *Educational Leadership, 60*(5), 70–73.

Center for Effective Collaboration and Practice. (2001). *Appendix B. Positive behavioral intervention plan: Planning form–Blank.* Retrieved from http://cecp.air.org/fba/problembehavior3/appendixb.htm

Chambers, A. C. (1997). *Has technology been considered?: A guide for IEP teams.* Reston, VA: Council for Exceptional Children.

Cihak, D. F., & Bowlin, T. (2010). Classroom management. In R. T. Boon & V. G. Spencer (Eds.), *Best practices for the inclusive classroom* (pp. 111–133). Waco, TX: Prufrock Press.

Conderman, G., & Johnston-Rodriguez, S. (2009). Beginning teachers' views of their collaborative roles. *Preventing School Failure, 53,* 235–244.

Conroy, M. A., Sutherland, K. S., Snyder, A. L., & Marsh, S. (2008). Classwide interventions: Effective instruction makes a difference. *TEACHING Exceptional Children, 40*(6), 24–30.

Cook, L., & Friend, M. (1993). Educational leadership for teacher collaboration. In B. S. Billingsley, D. Peterson, D. Bodkins, & M. B. Hendricks (Eds.), *Program leadership for serving students with disabilities* (pp. 421–444). (ERIC Document Reproduction Service No. ED372532)

De La Paz, S., & Graham, S. (1995). Dictation: Applications to writing for students with learning disabilities. In T. E. Scruggs & M. A. Mastropieri (Eds.), *Advances in learning and behavioral disabilities* (Vol. 9, pp. 227–247). Greenwich, CT: JAI Press.

deBettencourt, L. U., & Howard, L. A. (2007). *The effective special education teacher: A practical guide for success.* Upper Saddle River, NJ: Prentice Hall.

Dotson, R. K., & Henderson, M. (2009). Using student portfolios to guide instruction. *Illinois Reading Council Journal, 37*(4), 14–19.

Education for All Handicapped Children Act of 1975, Pub. Law 94-142 (November 29, 1975).

Edyburn, D. L. (2000). 1999 in review: A synthesis of the special education technology literature. *Journal of Special Education Technology, 15,* 7–18.

emTech. (n.d.). *Alternative/performance-based assessment.* Retrieved from http://www.emtech.net/Alternative_Assessment.html

Farmer, T. W., Goforth, J., Hives, J., Aaron, A., Hunter, F., & Sgmatto, A. (2006). Competence enhancement behavior management. *Preventing School Failure, 50,* 39–44.

Formal and informal assessments. (2006). Retrieved from http://www.associatedcontent.com/article/51770/formal_and_informal_assessments.html?cat=4

Friend, M., & Cook, L. (2007). *Interactions: Collaboration skills for school professionals* (5th ed.). Boston, MA: Allyn & Bacon.

Fuchs, L. S., & Fuchs, D. (1986). Effects of systematic formative evaluation: A meta-analysis. *Exceptional Children, 53,* 199–208.

Fuchs, D., & Fuchs, L. S. (1995). What's "special" about special education? A field under siege. *Phi Delta Kappan, 76,* 522–530.

Fuchs, L. S., Deno, S. L., & Mirkin, P. K. (1984). The effects of frequent curriculum-based measurement and evaluation on pedagogy, student achievement, and student awareness of learning. *American Educational Research Journal, 21,* 449–460.

Funderstanding. (n.d.). *Portfolio assessment.* Retrieved from http://www.funderstanding.com/content/portfolio-assessment

Ganz, J. B. (2008). Self-monitoring across age and ability levels: Teaching students to implement their own positive behavioral interventions. *Preventing School Failure, 53,* 39–48.

Gearhart, M., & Osmundson, E. (2009). Assessment portfolios as opportunities for teacher learning. *Educational Assessment, 14,* 1–24.

Gehrke, R. S., & McCoy, K. (2007). Considering the context: Differences between the environments of beginning special educators who stay and those who leave. *Rural Special Education Quarterly, 26*(3), 32–40.

Gerber, P. J., & Popp, P. A. (1999). Consumer perspectives on the collaborative teaching model. *Remedial and Special Education, 20,* 288–296.

Gersten, R., Keating, T., & Yovanoff, P. (2001). Working in special education: Factors that enhance special educators' intent to stay. *Exceptional Children, 67,* 549–567.

Gunter, P. L. (2001). Data-based decision making to ensure positive outcomes for children/youth with challenging behaviors. In L. M. Bullock & R. A. Gable (Eds.), *Addressing social, academic, and behavioral needs within inclusive and alternative settings* (pp. 49–52). Reston, VA: Council for Exceptional Children.

Gunter, P. L., Callicott, K., Denny, R. K., & Gerber, B. L. (2003). Finding a place for data collection in classrooms for students with emotional/behavioral disorders. *Preventing School Failure, 48,* 4–8.

Hagan-Burke, S., & Jefferson, G. L. (2002). Using data to promote academic benefit for included students with mild disabilities. *Preventing School Failure, 46,* 112–118.

Idol, L., Nevin, A., & Paolucci-Whitcomb, P. (1994). *Collaborative consultation* (2nd ed.). Austin, TX: PRO-ED.

Individuals with Disabilities Education Act, 20 U.S.C. §1401 et seq. (1990).

Individuals with Disabilities Education Act, PL 105-17, 111 Stat. 37 (1997).

Individuals with Disabilities Education Improvement Act, Pub. Law 108-446 (December 3, 2004).

Inge, K. J., & Shepard, J. (1995). Assistive technology applications and strategies for school system personnel. In K. F. Flippo, K. J. Inge, & J. M. Barcus (Eds.), *Assistive technology: A resource for school, work, and community* (pp. 133–166). Baltimore, MD: Brookes.

Isaacs, M. L. (2003). Data-driven decision-making: The engine of accountability. *Professional School Counseling, 6,* 288–295.

Jairrels, V. (1999). Cultural diversity: Implications for collaboration. *Intervention in School and Clinic, 34,* 236–238.

Jitendra, K., Edwards, L. L., Choutka, C. M., & Treadway, P. S. (2002). A collaborative approach to planning in the content area for students with learning disabilities: Accessing the general curriculum. *Learning Disabilities Research & Practice, 17,* 252–267.

Joyce, B., & Showers, B. (2002). *Student achievement through staff development* (3rd ed.). Alexandria, VA: Association for Supervision and Curriculum Development.

Kauffman, J. M., Mostert, M. P., Trent, S. C., & Pullen, P. L. (2006). *Managing classroom behavior: A reflective case-based approach* (4th ed.). Boston, MA: Allyn & Bacon.

Kelker, K. A., & Holt, R. (2000). *Family guide to assistive technology.* Cambridge, MA: Brookline Books.

King, T. W. (1999). *Assistive technology: Essential human factors.* Boston, MA: Allyn & Bacon.

Layton, C. A., & Lock, R. H. (2008). *Assessing students with special needs to produce quality outcomes.* Upper Saddle River, NJ: Merrill.

Leatherman, J. (2009). Teachers' voices concerning collaborative teams within an inclusive elementary school. *Teaching Education, 20,* 189–202.

Lerner, J. (2002). *Learning disabilities: Theories, diagnosis, and teaching strategies* (9th ed.). Boston, MA: Houghton Mifflin.

Lewis, R. (1993). *Special education technology: Classroom applications.* Pacific Grove, CA: Brooks/Cole.

Lindsey, J. D. (2000). *Technology and exceptional individuals* (3rd ed.). Austin, TX: Pro-Ed.

Lopez, C. L. (2002). Assessment of student learning: Challenges and strategies. *Journal of Academic Librarianship, 28,* 356–367.

Madaus, G. F., Kellaghan, T., Rakow, E. A., & King, D. J. (1979). The sensitivity of measures of school effectiveness. *Harvard Educational Review, 49,* 207–230.

Male, M. (2003). *Technology for inclusion. Meeting the special needs of all students* (4th ed.). Boston, MA: Allyn & Bacon.

Maryville City Schools. (2005). *IDEA categories.* Retrieved from http://www.ci.maryville.tn.us/mhs/MCSsped/IDEAcat.htm

Marzano, R. J. (2003). Using data: Two wrongs and a right. *Educational Leadership, 60*(5), 56–60.

Mastropieri, M. A., & Scruggs, T. E. (2010). *The inclusive classroom: Strategies for effective differentiated instruction* (4th ed.). Upper Saddle River, NJ: Pearson.

McMillan, J. H. (2007). *Classroom assessment: Principles and practice for effective standards-based instruction* (4th ed.). Boston, MA: Pearson.

McTighe, J., & Thomas, R. S. (2003). Backward design for forward action. *Educational Leadership, 60*(5), 52–55.

Meinick, S., & Meister, D. (2008). A comparison of beginning and experienced teachers' concerns. *Educational Research Quarterly, 31*(3), 39–45.

Melichair, J. F., & Blackhurst, A. E. (1993). *Introduction to a functional approach to assistive technology* [Training Module]. Lexington: University of Kentucky Department of Special Education and Rehabilitation Counseling.

National Association of Special Education Teachers. (n.d.). *Assessment in special education series.* Retrieved from http://www.naset.org/2876.0.html

National Capital Language Resource Center. (n.d.). *Assessing learning: Peer and self assessment.* Retrieved from http://www.nclrc.org/essentials/assessing/peereval.htm

National Center for Education Statistics. (2006). *Fast facts.* http://nces.ed.gov/fastfacts/display.asp?id=59

National Research Council. (2003). *Evaluating and improving undergraduate teaching in science, technology, engineering, and mathematics.* Washington, DC: National Academy Press.

No Child Left Behind Act, 20 U.S.C. §6301 (2001).

Norrell, L. (1997). A case for responsible inclusion. *Teaching Pre-K–8, 28,* 17.

Office of Technology Assessment of the U.S. Congress. (1995). *Education and technology: Future visions.* Retrieved from http://www.princeton.edu/~ota/disk1/1995/9522/9522.PDF

Oortwijn, M. B., Boekaerts, M., & Vedder, P. (2008). The effect of stimulating immigrant and national pupils' helping behavior during cooperative learning in classrooms on their math-related talk. *Educational Studies, 34,* 333–342.

Overton, T. (2006). *Assessing learners with special needs* (5th ed.). Upper Saddle River, NJ: Merrill.

Parette, H. P. (1998). Effective and promising assistive technology practices for students with mental retardation and developmental disabilities. In A. Hilton & R. Ringlaben (Eds.), *Effective and promising practices in developmental disabilities* (pp. 205–224*)*. Austin, TX: PRO-ED.

Parette, H. P., & Angelo, D. H. (1996). Augmentative and alternative communication impact on families: Trends and future directions. *The Journal of Special Education, 30,* 77–98.

Parette, H. P., & Brotherson, M. J. (1996). Family participation in assistive technology assessment for young children with disabilities. *Education and Training in Mental Retardation and Developmental Disabilities, 31,* 29–43.

Parette, H. P., & Hourcade, J. J. (1997). Family issues and assistive technology needs: A sampling of state practices. *Journal of Special Education Technology, 13*(3), 27–43.

Pierangelo, R., & Giuliani, G. A. (2006). *Assessment in special education: A practical approach* (2nd ed.). Boston, MA: Pearson.

Plash, S., & Piotrowski, C. (2006). Retention issues: A study of Alabama special education teachers. *Education, 127,* 125–128.

Polloway, E. A., Patton, J. R., & Serna, L. (2008). *Strategies for teaching learners with special needs* (9th ed.). Upper Saddle River, NJ: Prentice Hall.

Project Appleseed. (n.d.). *What should parents know about performance based assessment?* Retrieved from http://www.projectappleseed.org/assesment.html

Ritter, J., & Hancock, D. (2007). Exploring the relationship between certification sources, experience levels, and classroom management orientations of classroom teachers. *Teaching and Teacher Education: An International Journal of Research and Studies, 23,* 1206–1216.

Roberts, J. L., & Inman, T. F. (2009). *Strategies for differentiating instruction: Best practices for the classroom* (2nd ed.). Waco, TX: Prufrock Press.

Rogers, E. M. (1995). *Diffusion of innovations* (4th ed.). New York, NY: The Free Press.

Rolheiser, C., & Ross, J. A. (n.d.). *Student self-evaluation: What research says and what practice shows.* Retrieved from http://www.cdl.org/resource-library/articles/self_eval.php

Romeo, L. (2008). Informal writing assessment linked to instruction: A continuous process for teachers, students, and parents. *Reading & Writing Quarterly, 24,* 25–51.

Saddler, B., & Graham, S. (2005). The effects of peer-assisted sentence-combining instruction on the writing performance of more and less skilled young writers. *Journal of Educational Psychology, 97,* 43–54.

Salend, S. J. (2005). *Creating inclusive classrooms: Effective and reflective practices* (5th ed.). Upper Saddle River, NJ: Merrill.

Salvia, J., Ysseldyke, J. E., & Bolt, S. (2007). *Assessment in special and inclusive education* (10th ed.). Boston, MA: Houghton Mifflin.

Section 504 of the Rehabilitation Act, 29 U.S.C. Section 706 et. Seq. (1973).

Shinn, M. R. (1997). *Exploring and evaluating solutions.* Eugene: University of Oregon, Curriculum-Based Measurement and Problem-Solving Institute, CBM Network.

Shinn, M. R., Habedank, L., & Good, R. H. (1993). The effects of classroom reading performance data on general education teachers' and parents' attitudes about reintegration. *Exceptionality, 4,* 205–228.

Silverman, S. M., & Weinfeld, R. (2007). *School success for kids with Asperger's syndrome.* Waco, TX: Prufrock Press.

Simpson, C. G., & Warner, L. (2010). *Successful inclusion strategies for early childhood teachers.* Waco, TX: Prufrock Press.

Slobodzian, J. T. (2009). The devil is in the details: Issues of exclusion in an inclusive educational environment. *Ethnography and Education, 4,* 181–195.

Smith, R., Benge, M., & Hall, M. (1994). Technology for self-care. In C. Christiansen (Ed.), *Ways of living: Self-care strategies for special needs* (pp. 379–422). Rockville, MD: American Occupational Therapy Association.

Spencer, V. G. (2006). Peer tutoring and students with emotional or behavioral disorders: A review of the literature. *Behavioral Disorders, 31,* 204–222.

Spencer, V. G., Scruggs, T. E., & Mastropieri, M. A. (2003). Content area learning in middle school social studies classrooms and students with emotional or behavioral disorders: A comparison of strategies. *Behavioral Disorders, 28*(2), 77–93.

Spencer, V. G., Simpson, C. G., & Oatis, T. (2009). An update on the use of peer tutoring and students with emotional and behavioral disorders. *Exceptionality Education International, 19,* 2–13.

Spraker, J. (2003). *Teacher teaming in relation to student performance: Findings from the literature.* Portland, OR: Northwest Regional Educational Laboratory.

Sutherland, K. S. (2000). Promoting positive interactions between teachers and students with emotional/behavioral disorders. *Preventing School Failure, 44,* 110–115.

Tawney, J. W., & Gast, D. (1984). *Single subject research in special education.* Columbus, OH: Merrill.

Technology-Related Assistance for Individuals with Disabilities Act, PL 100-407 (1988).

Texas Council for Developmental Disabilities. (n.d.). *People first language.* Retrieved from http://www.txddc.state.tx.us/resources/publications/pfanguage. asp

Thornton, B., Peltier, G., & Medina, R. (2007). Reducing the special education teacher shortage. *The Clearing House, 80,* 233–238.

Tomlinson, C. (1995). *Differentiating instruction for mixed-ability classrooms.* Alexandria, VA: ASCD.

U.S. Department of Education. (2007a). *The condition of education 2007.* Washington, DC: Author.

U.S. Department of Education. (2007b). *Twenty-seventh annual report to Congress on the implementation of IDEA.* Washington, DC: Author.

Venn, J. J. (2000). *Assessing students with special needs* (2nd ed.). Upper Saddle River, NJ: Merrill.

Villa, R. A., Thousand, J. S., Nevin, A. I., & Malgeri, C. (1996). Instilling collaboration for inclusive schooling as a way of doing business in public schools. *Remedial and Special Education, 17,* 169–181.

Voltz, D. L., & Collins, L. (2010). Preparing special education administrators for inclusion in diverse, standards-based contexts: Beyond the Council for Exceptional Children and the interstate school leaders licensure consortium. *Teacher Education and Special Education, 33,* 70–82.

Weinfeld, R., & Davis, M. (2008). *Special needs advocacy resource book: What you can do now to advocate for your exceptional child's education.* Waco, TX: Prufrock Press.

Worrell, J. L. (2008). How secondary schools can avoid the seven deadly sins of inclusion. *American Secondary Education, 36,* 43–56.

Zabala, J. (2002). *Update of the SETT framework, 2002.* Retrieved from http://www.joyzabala.com

Appendix A

Due Process

We will discuss the numerous features of due process in this appendix. Each of these features is important for the classroom teacher to understand, as he may be directly impacted if a due process is enacted. These include:

- procedural safeguards notice,
- statute of limitations,
- due process complaint notice,
- resolutions, and
- attorney fees.

Procedural Safeguards Notice

The procedural safeguards notice (written brochure) will be distributed once a year, except that a copy will also be distributed upon initial referral, when a parent makes a request for an evaluation, when a due process complaint has been filed, or if a parent requests a copy. As a classroom teacher, it is worth your time to read over the procedural safeguards that are issued to parents. You should have the same knowledge as the parents do about the rights of their children in your classroom.

Statute of Limitations

Parents now have 2 years in which to exercise their due process rights after they knew or should have known that an IDEA violation has occurred. The interpretation of the language "should have known" will be critical. Basically, this means that if you served a child a year ago in your classroom and a parent deems a year later that IDEA was violated during the time in which the child received services in the inclusive classroom, you would likely be part of the due process hearing if it occurs. We recommend that you maintain documentation on students for this particular reason.

Due Process Complaint Notice

Parents who feel their child's educational rights are being compromised must file a complaint with the school district (with a copy to the state), identifying the name and contact information of the child and describing the nature of the problem with supporting facts and a proposed resolution. A new provision provides that the school district shall file a response within 10 days unless the district notifies the state hearing officer within 15 days that it is challenging the sufficiency of the parent's due process complaint notice. The state hearing officer has 5 more days to make a finding. A parent may or may not make you aware that he will be filing a due process request. Often, teachers are caught off guard when an initial complaint is filed.

Resolution Session

Parents must go through a mandatory resolution session before due process begins. The school district will convene a meeting with the parents and relevant members of the IEP team (more than likely you, as the classroom teacher, will be involved in this process) within 15 days of when the school district receives the parent's due process complaint. The school district has 30 days from the time the request is filed to resolve the complaint to the satisfaction of the parents, after which a due process hearing can occur. This provision may encourage school systems to wait until a due process complaint is filed before trying to resolve issues. Attorney fees are not reimbursed for work related to the resolution session.

Attorney Fees

Parents' attorneys may be responsible for paying the school system's attorney fees if a cause of action in a due process hearing or court action is determined to be frivolous, unreasonable, or without foundation. Parents may be responsible for the school system's attorney fees if a cause of action was presented for any improper purpose such as to harass or to cause unnecessary delay or needless increase in the cost of litigation. Obviously, parents should not file frivolous or improper causes of action, but it is important that school districts not use these changes in the law to intimidate parents. This could have a chilling effect on parents obtaining legal representation and filing valid complaints to improve their children's education.

Timelines for Due Process

When due process comes into play, there are certain guidelines that must be followed. The due process complaint must allege a violation that occurred not more than 2 years before the date the parent or public agency knew or should have known about the alleged action that forms the basis of the due process complaint, or it needs to be filed based on the state guidelines if the state has an explicit time limitation for filing a due process request. Also, a parent or agency must request an impartial hearing on the due process complaint within this 2-year limit.

With regard to procedures, the public agency must have procedures that require either party, or the attorney representing a party, to provide to the other party a request for a due process complaint (which must remain confidential). The party filing a due process request must forward a copy of it to the state educational agency (SEA). It must include:

- the name of the child;
- the address of the residence of the child;
- the name of the school the child is attending;
- in the case of a homeless child or youth, available contact information for the child and the name of the school the child is attending;
- a description of the nature of the problem of the child relating to the proposed or refused initiation or change, including facts relating to the problem; and
- a proposed resolution of the problem to the extent known and available to the party at the time.

The due process complaint must be deemed sufficient unless the party receiving it notifies the hearing officer and the other party in writing, within 15 days of receipt of the due process complaint, that the receiving party believes it does not meet the requirements.

If the local education agency (LEA) has not sent a prior written notice to the parent regarding the subject matter contained in the parent's due process complaint, the LEA must, within 10 days of receiving the due process request, send to the parent a response that includes:

- an explanation of why the agency proposed or refused to take the action raised in the due process complaint;
- a description of other options that the IEP team considered and the reasons why those options were rejected;
- a description of each evaluation procedure, assessment, record, or report the agency used as the basis for the proposed or refused action; and

- a description of the other factors that are relevant to the agency's proposed or refused action.

When a due process complaint is filed, the party receiving it must, within 10 days of receiving the request, send to the other party a response that specifically addresses the issues raised in the complaint. Within 5 days of receipt of notification, the hearing officer must make a determination of whether the due process complaint meets the requirements and must immediately notify the parties in writing of that determination.

Within 15 days of receiving notice of the parent's due process complaint, and prior to the initiation of a due process hearing, the LEA must convene a meeting with the parent and the relevant member or members of the IEP team who have specific knowledge of the facts identified in the due process request. That meeting should include a representative of the public agency who has decision-making authority on behalf of that agency and may not include an attorney of the LEA unless the parent is accompanied by an attorney. The purpose of the meeting is for the parent of the child to discuss the complaint, and the facts that form the basis of it, so that the LEA has the opportunity to resolve the dispute.

If the LEA has not resolved the due process complaint to the satisfaction of the parent within 30 days of its receipt, the due process hearing may occur. If the LEA is unable to obtain the participation of the parent in the resolution meeting after reasonable efforts have been made (and documented), the LEA may, at the conclusion of the 30-day period, request that a hearing officer dismiss the parent's due process complaint. If the LEA fails to hold the resolution meeting within 15 days of receiving notice of a parent's due process request or fails to participate in the resolution meeting, the parent may seek the intervention of a hearing officer to begin the due process hearing timeline. The party requesting the due process hearing may not raise issues at the hearing that were not raised in the complaint filed, unless the other party agrees otherwise.

Whenever a hearing is requested, the parents or the LEA involved in the dispute must have an opportunity for an impartial due process hearing. The SEA or LEA is responsible for arranging the expedited due process hearing, which must occur within 20 school days of the date the complaint requesting the hearing is filed. The hearing officer must make a determination within 10 school days after the hearing. Unless the parents and LEA agree in writing to waive the resolution meeting or agree to use the mediation process, a resolution meeting must occur within 7 days of receiving notice of the due process complaint and the due process hearing may proceed unless the matter has been resolved to the satisfaction of both parties within 15 days of the receipt of the complaint. We must also note that the decisions on expedited due process hearings are appealable.

Appendix B

Sample IEP Forms

THE INDIVIDUALIZED EDUCATION PROGRAM FOR:		
Name: First	**Middle**	**Last**
Birth Date: **Age:**	**Student ID:**	
Present Grade Level:	**School:**	
Primary Language or Communication Mode(s): ❑ English ❑ Spanish ❑ sign language ❑ other (specify) _____		
IEP Type: ❑ Initial ❑ Annual Date of Most Recent Evaluation/Reevaluation: Date of Previous IEP Review: Projected Date for Next Triennial Evaluation:		
IEP CONTENT (Required):		
Date of IEP Meeting:	Initiation Date of IEP:	
Projected Date of Annual IEP Review:	Parent(s)/Legal Guardian(s) Provided Copy of This IEP:	
PARTICIPANTS IN IEP MEETING AND ROLE(S) The names and roles of individuals participating in developing the IEP meeting must be documented.		
Name of Person and Role Signatures are not required. If a signature is used it only indicates attendance, not agreement.		**Method of Attendance**
	Parent/Guardian	
	Parent/Guardian	
	Student	
	LEA Representative	❑ in person ❑ excused ❑ in writing (if applicable)
	Special Education Teacher	❑ in person ❑ excused ❑ in writing (if applicable)
	Regular Classroom Teacher	❑ in person ❑ excused ❑ in writing (if applicable)
	Individual Interpreting Instructional Implications of Evaluation Results	❑ in person ❑ excused ❑ in writing (if applicable)
	Part C Representative (if applicable)	
	Representative of an Agency That May Provide Postsecondary Transition Services (if applicable)	
	Other:	

Student Name:	Date of IEP:

Present Level of Academic Achievement and Functional Performance

Present Level must include:

✓ How the child's disability affects his or her involvement and progress in the general education curriculum; or for preschool children, participation in age-appropriate activities

For students with transition plans, consider how the child's disability will affect the child's ability to reach his or her postsecondary goals (what the child will do after high school).

_____

_____

✓ The strengths of the child

For students with transition plans, consider how the strengths of the child relate to the child's postsecondary goals.

_____

_____

✓ Concerns of the parent/guardian for enhancing the education of the child

For students with transition plans, consider the parent/guardian's expectations for the child after the child leaves high school.

_____

_____

✓ Changes in current functioning of the child since the initial or prior IEP

For students with transition plans, consider how changes in the child's current functioning will impact the child's ability to reach his or her postsecondary goal.

_____

_____

✓ A summary of the most recent evaluation/reevaluation results

_____

_____

✓ A summary of the results of the child's performance on:

   o Formal or informal age appropriate transition assessments

_____

_____

✓ For students participating in alternative assessments, a description of benchmarks or short-term objectives

   o N/A Objectives/benchmarks are on goal page(s)

   o Objectives/benchmarks described below:

_____

_____

_____

_____

_____

_____

Student Name:	Date of IEP:

Special Considerations: Federal and State Requirements

Note: For the first six items below, if the IEP team determines that the child needs a particular device or service (including an intervention, accommodation, or other program modification) information documenting the team's decision regarding the device or service must be included in the appropriate section of the IEP. These must be considered annually.

Is the student blind or visually impaired?
❑ No
❑ Yes

Is the student deaf or hearing impaired?
❑ No
❑ Yes. The IEP team has considered the child's language and communication needs, opportunities for direct communication with peers and professionals in the child's language and communication mode, academic level, and full range of needs including opportunities for direct instruction in the child's language and communication mode in the development of the IEP.

Does the student exhibit behaviors that impede his or her learning or that of others?
❑ No
❑ Yes. If yes, strategies including positive behavior interventions and supports must be considered by the IEP team, and if determined necessary, addressed in this IEP. If a behavior intervention plan is developed it must be a part of the IEP.

Does the student have limited English proficiency?
❑ No
❑ Yes. The student's language needs are addressed in this IEP.

Does the student have communication needs?
❑ No
❑ Yes. The student's communication needs are addressed in this IEP.

Does the student require assistive technology device(s) and/or services?
❑ No
❑ Yes. The student's assistive technology needs are addressed in this IEP.

Extended School Year (ESY):
❑ No. The student is not eligible for ESY services.
❑ Yes. The student is eligible for ESY services.

Transfer of Rights: Notification must be given beginning not later than one year before the student is 18 informing the student of the rights under IDEA that will transfer to the student upon reaching the age of majority.
❑ N/A for this student/IEP
❑ Notification was given: (month/day/year)

State Assessments
IDEA requires students with disabilities to participate in state assessments. This is specific to the district.

Districtwide Assessments
Are there districtwide assessments administered for this student's age/grade level? If yes, additional paperwork will be required.
❑ No
❑ Yes

Postsecondary Transition Services: (Must be included not later than the first IEP to be in effect when the child turns 16, and updated annually thereafter.)
Is a Postsecondary Transition Plan required?
❑ No (Child will not turn 16 while this IEP is in effect.)
❑ Yes (Child is/will be 16 while this IEP is in effect.). If yes, additional paperwork is required.

Student Name:					Date of IEP:			

Annual Goals and Objectives

Annual Goal:	By:

Report of Student Progress: ❑ Monthly ❑ Quarterly ❑ Yearly ❑ Other

Progress of Goals:	1	2	3	4	5	6	7	8
Date of Review:								
Progress Toward Goal:								

Progress on this goal will be reported using the following codes:

✓ ES: **Emerging Skill** demonstrated but may not achieve annual goal within duration of IEP.

✓ IP: **Insufficient Progress** demonstrated to meet this annual goal and may not achieve annual goal within duration of IEP.

✓ M: **Mastered** this annual goal.

✓ NI: **Not** been provided **Instruction** on this goal

What types of accommodations, if any, are necessary for the student to make effective progress?

_____
_____
_____
_____

Short Term Objectives or Benchmarks

Objective 1: By _____, _____ will _____

Comments: Last Updated: _____

Mastery Criteria: _____

Evaluation Method: _____

Other Evaluation Method: _____

Objective 2: By _____, _____ will _____

Comments: Last Updated: _____

Mastery Criteria: _____

Evaluation Method: _____

Other Evaluation Method: _____

Student Name:	Date of IEP:

Reporting Progress

When Progress will be reported to the parent(s)/guardian(s):
❑ Quarterly   ❑ Bi-Quarterly   ❑ Semester   ❑ Annually   ❑ Other: _____

Services Summary

Special Education Services	
Related Services: ❑ N/A	
Supplementary Aids/Services: ❑ N/A	

Transportation as a Related Service

❑ The student **does not** require transportation as a related service.
❑ The student requires transportation as a necessary related service.
     The student needs accommodations or modifications for transportation.
     ❑ No   ❑ Yes
     If yes, check any transportation accommodations/modifications that are needed.
     ❑ Wheelchair lift
     ❑ Child safety restraint system. Specify: _____
     ❑ Door-to-door pick up and drop off
     ❑ Aide
     ❑ Other. Specify: _____

Regular Education Participation

Extent of Participation in Regular Education

For Preschool: Will all of this child's special education and related services be provided with nondisabled peers in a regular education setting (designed primarily for children without disabilities)?
❑ Yes.
❑ No. If no:
     a. To what extent will the child not receive special education and related services in a regular educa-tion setting (minutes or % of special education and related service minutes on the IEP)?

     _____

     b. Describe the reasons why the IEP team determined that provision of services in the regular educa-tion setting was not appropriate. _____

     _____

For K–12: The regular education environment includes all academic instruction as well as meals, recess, assemblies, field trips, etc. Will this student participate 100% of the time with nondisabled peers in the regular education environment?
❑ Yes.
❑ No. If no, describe below to what extent the student will not participate **and** why full participation is not appropriate.
(Child's name) _____ will participate in regular education _____% of the time.
Full participation in regular education is not appropriate because _____

_____

Student Name:	Date of IEP:

Placement Considerations and Decisions

This section is a SUMMARY of all of the following: Present Level of Academic Achievement and Functional Performance, goals, objectives/benchmarks (if applicable), characteristics of services, adaptations, and special education and related services information.

Annual Consideration of Placement

✓ **For Preschool**: At least annually the IEP team must consider whether all of the special education and related services will be provided with nondisabled peers in a regular education setting (designed primarily for children without disabilities).

✓ **For K–12**: At least annually, the IEP team must consider if the IEP goals can be met with services provided 100% of the time in the regular education environment.

✓ Check **all** placement options that were **considered** for the provision of special education and related services. (For K–12, Inside regular class at least 80% of time must be checked. For preschool, early childhood [EC] setting must be checked).

✓ Check the **one** placement option that was selected.

Placement Continuum (K–12)

	Considered	Selected	
1.	❏	❏	Inside regular class at least 80% of time
2.	❏	❏	Inside regular class 40% to 79% of time
3.	❏	❏	Inside regular class less than 40% of time
4.	❏	❏	Public separate school (day) facility
5.	❏	❏	Private separate school (day) facility
6.	❏	❏	Public residential facility
7.	❏	❏	Private residential facility
8.	❏	❏	Homebound/hospital

Placement Options (EC)

	Considered	Selected	
1.	❏	❏	Early childhood setting
2.	❏	❏	Early childhood special education
3.	❏	❏	Home
4.	❏	❏	Part-time early childhood/Part-time early childhood special education
5.	❏	❏	Residential facility
6.	❏	❏	Separate school
7.	❏	❏	Itinerant service outside the home

For K–12 students:

Is this student's placement as close as possible to the child's home and/or in the school he/she would attend if nondisabled?

❏ Yes.

❏ No. If no, explain why another school/setting is required. _____

_____

_____

_____

Appendix C

Scatter Plot Assessment Tool

Date: **6/21/09**   Name of Person Observed: **John Smith**   Observer: **Ms. Classroom Teacher**

Behavior(s): **throwing books, out of seat**

Directions: At the end of each time interval, fill in the square indicating the appropriate time and date on the chart using the code given below:

		⊠ Throwing Books			◹ Out of Seat			
Time								
8:30	*Math*							
9:00			⊠	⊠	⊠	⊠		
9:30	*Science*							
10:00		◹		◹		⊠		
10:30								
11:00	*Reading/Writing*	⊠		◹			◹	
11:30								
12:00	*Lunch*							
12:30								
1:00	*P.E./Art*							
1:30								
2:00	*Social Studies*		◹	◹			◹		◹
2:30								
3:00	*Clean up*							
3:30								
Date		6/20	6/21	6/22	6/23	6/24	6/27	6/28	6/29

Appendix D

Blank Scatter Plot Assessment Tool

Date: _____ Name of Person Observed: _____ Observer: _____

Behavior(s): _____

Directions: At the end of each time interval, fill in the square indicating the appropriate time and date on the chart using the code given below:

Time									
	Date								

Appendix E

Completed ABC Chart

Child's Name: __Thomas__

Observer: __Ms. Spencer__

Environment: __Playground__

Date: __4/22/08__

Observation Start Time: __2:30 p.m.__

Observation Stop Time: __2:45 p.m.__

Antecedent Events	Observed Behavior	Consequent Events
2:36: Students are running around in a circle.	Thomas pushed Lee from behind.	Lee turned around and yelled at Thomas to stop.
2:42: Students are standing in a group and talking.	Thomas told Lee, "You're a jerk," and hit him on the arm.	Lee said nothing and did nothing. Thomas smiled and walked away.
2:45: Bell rings for kids to return to classroom. Kids begin to run toward building.	Thomas hit Lee on the back as the two were running toward the building.	Lee continued to run toward the building. Lee did not give Thomas a response. Thomas laughed.

Appendix F

Blank ABC Chart

Child's Name: _____

Observer: _____

Environment: _____

Date: _____

Observation Start Time: _____

Observation Stop Time: _____

Antecedent Events	Observed Behavior	Consequent Events

Sample Behavior Intervention Plan

Directions: IEP teams can use this form to guide them through the process of developing the Positive Behavioral Intervention Plan.

Student:
Age:
Sex:
Teacher:
Grade:
Case Manager:
Date:

Behavior(s)	
1. Problem behavior: Define the problem behavior(s) in observable, measurable, and countable terms (i.e., topography, event, duration, seriousness, and/or intensity). Include several examples of the behavior.	
2. Identify likely antecedents (precipitating events) to the behavior(s).	
3. Identify likely consequences that may be maintaining the behavior(s).	
4. Identify and describe any academic or environmental context(s) in which the problem behavior(s) does not occur.	
5. Describe replacement behavior(s) that are likely to serve the same function as the behavior(s).	

Methods of measuring	
1. Describe how data will be measured (e.g., permanent products, event recording, scatter plot), and when and where student behavior(s) occurred.	
2. Summarize data by specifying which problem behavior(s) and replacement behavior(s) will be targets for intervention.	

Behavioral intervention plan	
1. Specify goals and objectives (i.e., conditions, criteria for acceptable performance) for teaching the replacement behavior(s).	
2. Specify instructional strategies that will be used to teach the replacement behavior(s).	
3. Specify strategies that will be used to decrease problem behavior(s) and increase replacement behavior(s).	
4. Identify any changes in the physical environment needed to prevent problem behavior(s) and to promote desired (replacement) behavior(s), if necessary.	
5. Specify the extent to which the intervention plan will be implemented in various settings; specify settings and persons responsible for implementation of plan.	

Evaluation plan and schedule	
1. Describe the plan and timetable to evaluate effectiveness of the intervention plan.	
2. Describe how, when, where, and how often the problem behavior(s) will be measured.	
3. Specify persons and settings involved.	
4. Specify a plan for crisis/emergency intervention, if necessary.	
5. Determine schedule to review/modify the intervention plan, as needed. Include dates and criteria for changing/fading the plan.	

Describe plan and timetable to monitor the degree to which the plan is being implemented:

_____

_____

_____

_____

_____

_____

_____

_____

_____

_____

Adapted from Center for Effective Collaboration and Practice (2001).

Appendix H

Basic ABC Data Form

Student: _____

Observer: _____

Behavior: _____

Date	Time	Antecedent	Behavior	Consequence

Appendix

Event Recording Data Sheet

Student: _____

Observer: _____

Behavior: _____

Date	Start Time	Stop Time	Number of Occurrences	Total Occurrences

Appendix J

Duration Recording Data Sheet

Student: _____

Observer: _____

Behavior: _____

Initiation: _____

Termination: _____

Date	Start Time	Stop Time	Total Duration	Average Duration

Latency Recording Data Sheet

Student: _____

Observer: _____

Behavior: _____

Date	Time of Instruction/ Teacher Directive	Time Student Begins Response	Total Latency	Average Latency

About the Authors

Cynthia G. Simpson, Ph.D., is associate professor of special education, Department of Language, Literacy and Special Populations at Sam Houston State University in Huntsville, TX. She has a bachelor's degree in elementary education from Texas State University-San Marcos, a masters of education from Sam Houston State University, and her doctoral degree from Texas A&M University. Dr. Simpson holds Educational Diagnostician (PK–12), Supervision (PK–12) Instructional Leadership Certification, Early Childhood Pre-Kindergarten/ Kindergarten (PK–12), English as a Second Language (PK–12), Generic Special Education (PK–12), and Self- Contained Elementary Education (1–8) certifications. Dr. Simpson is actively involved in the field of special education with specific areas of interest including transition, assessment, learning strategies, preschool inclusion, and nutrition and health issues of children with special needs. She has written more than 70 academic publications, including six books, journal articles, chapters, and proceedings, and she has made multiple presentations at the local, state, regional, national, and international levels. Dr. Simpson is the recipient of numerous awards and recognitions, including the 2010 Teacher Educator Award (Council for Exceptional Children, Texas Federation), 2009 Wilma Jo Bush Award (educational diagnostics), 2008 Susan Gorin Phillips Award (Council for Exceptional Children, Student Leadership), 2008 Kathleen Varner Service Award (Texas Council for Exceptional Children), and 2007 Susan Hargrave Trainer of the Year Award (Texas Association for the Education of Young

Children). Through her work, she has dedicated herself to improving services for students with exceptionalities and their families, as well as providing opportunities for individuals with special needs to be fully included in society at the academic and social levels. She is specifically focused on improving opportunities for individuals with special needs to attend postsecondary education.

Vicky Spencer, Ph.D., B.C.B.A–D, is currently associate professor in special education and the Assistant Director of Operations at the Kellar Institute for Human disAbilities at George Mason University in Fairfax, VA. She has a bachelor's degree in speech pathology and audiology from the University of Texas at Dallas, a masters degree in special education from Texas A & M–Commerce, and a doctoral degree from George Mason University in special education and literacy. Dr. Spencer also holds certification as an Educational Diagnostician, and she is also a Board Certified Behavior Analyst. Her research interests include cognitive strategy instruction, inclusive practices, and international research and teacher training. She has published four books, written numerous publications, and presents her research at educational conferences at the state, national, and international level. Dr. Spencer has been named as a Fulbright Scholar and will continue her ongoing work in special education program development in underdeveloped countries. She has served in the field of special education for more than 20 years focusing on teacher education and students with disabilities and will continue to pursue opportunities for expanding the education and services for people with disabilities worldwide.

Jeffrey P. Bakken, Ph.D., is professor and chair of the Department of Special Education at Illinois State University. He has a bachelor's degree in elementary education from the University of Wisconsin-LaCrosse and graduate degrees in the area of special education and learning disabilities from Purdue University. Dr. Bakken is a teacher, consultant, and scholar. His specific areas of interest include transition, teacher effectiveness, inclusion, learning strategies, collaboration, and technology. He has written more than 100 academic publications, including books, journal articles, chapters, monographs, reports, and proceedings, and he has made more than 200 presentations at the local, state, regional, national, and international levels. Dr. Bakken has received the College of Education and the University Research Initiative Award, the College of Education Outstanding College Researcher Award, the College of Education Outstanding College Teacher Award, and the Outstanding University Teacher Award from Illinois State University. Additionally, he is on the editorial boards of many scholarly publications, including *Multicultural Learning and Teaching*, *Remedial and Special Education*, and *Exceptional Children*. Through his work, he has committed himself to improving teachers' knowledge and techniques, as well as services for students with exceptionalities and their families.